"My friend and brother in Christ has given us a timely reflection on walking with a holy God. R. T., whom we proudly recognize as a graduate of Trevecca, blends careful exegesis with lived experience. This equals wisdom. In a world bent on seeking pleasure and seeking to please, we find guidance by realizing that in Christ we please the God who knit us together, called us by name, and poured his life into us. I pray that you may emerge from this book with a purer desire to please God."

—DAN BOONE, president, Trevecca Nazarene University

"Once again, Dr. Kendall has given us an updated and practical recipe for our Christian lives. The reader will find a new lens for the examination of our active faith. Thank you, R. T.!"

—JOHN DIXON, MD, Vanderbilt University School of Medicine

"R. T. Kendall is a gift to the body of Christ across the world. His newest book, *Pleasing God*, challenges me to live a life that prioritizes pleasing God above everything else. We need to share the much needed message of this book across the church and the world today. Please get a copy, read it, and encourage others to do the same."

—DR. RONNIE W. FLOYD, author, ministry strategist, and pastor emeritus, Cross Church

"As a child, I desired to please my father. Nothing seemed more important than putting a smile on his face and hearing him say, 'Well done.' Likewise, every Christian should desire to please his heavenly Father. In his new book *Pleasing God*, R. T. Kendall shares biblical steps to experience the Lord's pleasure. Read and apply it, and you'll experience God's affirming smile."

—PASTOR STEVE GAINES, PhD, Bellevue Baptist Church, Memphis, Tennessee

"In a virtual world of likes, shares, and retweets, the temptation to please others presses on us all the time. R. T. Kendall humbly guides us by offering a much-needed course correction for why we should and how we can please God. I've had the privilege of watching Dr. Kendall live out the pages of this book in his own life. Your intimacy with God will be deeper after reading this volume."

—ROBBY GALLATY, pastor, Long Hollow Church,
author of *Recovered and Growing Up*.

PLEASING
GOD

PLEASING GOD

THE GREATEST JOY AND HIGHEST HONOR

R. T. KENDALL

THOMAS NELSON
Since 1798

THOMAS NELSON

Pleasing God
© 2023 by R. T. Kendall

Published in Nashville, Tennessee, by Thomas Nelson. Thomas Nelson is a registered trademark of HarperCollins Christian Publishing, Inc.

Thomas Nelson titles may be purchased in bulk for educational, business, fundraising, or sales promotional use. For information, please e-mail SpecialMarkets@ ThomasNelson.com.

ISBN 978-0-310-15348-1 (audio)

Library of Congress Cataloging-in-Publication Data

Names: Kendall, R. T., 1935- author.
Title: Pleasing God: the greatest joy and highest honor / R. T. Kendall.
Description: Nashville, Tennessee: Thomas Nelson, 2023.
Identifiers: LCCN 2022060197 | ISBN 9780310153467 (paperback) | ISBN 9780310153474 (ebook)
Subjects: LCSH: God (Christianity) | God (Christianity)—Attributes. | Christian life.
Classification: LCC BT130 .K46 2023 | DDC 231/.4—dc23/eng/20230620
LC record available at https://lccn.loc.gov/2022060197

Cover design: Bruce Gore | Gore Studio, Inc.
Cover photo: © Vitalii Bashkatov / Shutterstock
Interior design: Sara Colley

Printed in the United States of America

23 24 25 26 27 28 29 30 31 32 /TRM/ 12 11 10 9 8 7 6 5 4 3 2 1

In memory of Ernie (1920–2016)
and Margaret Paddon (b. 1926)

Find out what pleases the Lord.

—EPHESIANS 5:10 NIV

He knows the way He taketh,
And I will walk with Him.

—ANNA L. WARING (1823–1910), "IN HEAVENLY LOVE ABIDING"

CONTENTS

FOREWORD

⟶ ✦

Once again, a significant work on the Christian life comes from the prolific pen of Dr. R. T. Kendall (whom I know as my friend R. T.). Using Enoch as an example, R. T. skillfully guides the reader into a deeper understanding of how to please God. This is a repeated theme in Scripture, especially encapsulated in Hebrews 11:6 (NIV): "Without faith it is impossible to please God . . ." To what kind of faith is the writer of Hebrews referring? How can it best be described? Is this faith simply a checklist of "dos" and "don'ts"? Or is this faith more about an attitude of the heart? Or a combination of both? In this book we explore the rich heritage of a vibrant biblical faith, drawing from R. T.'s insightful understanding of Scripture along with his life and ministry experiences over the past decades.

Throughout the history of the church, believers have sought ways to draw close to God, to find intimacy with him, and to please him. Some believers in the early church sought God's approval by living as hermits in the stark emptiness of the desert, believing that self-denial would increase his love for them. Medieval mystics often took up the ascetic life, depriving themselves of food, sleep, and any form of worldly comforts. Taking extreme vows of poverty, they believed these practices would earn additional approval from God. While these actions are bewildering to our Western minds, we can appreciate these saints' desire to please the Lord and their willingness to sacrifice for that purpose. But is God looking for these intense ways of living in his followers? What exactly does he expect from us?

We have a relationship with God—and relationships involve the will, the mind, the emotions, and the heart. All of these aspects are wrapped up in finding ways to be pleasing to him. As I read through this book, I am reminded that a large part of pleasing God means making an intentional effort to grow and discover what pleases him, so that we can testify as David did, "My soul follows close behind You. . . ." (Ps. 63:8 NKJV).

R. T. has stated that his purpose in writing this book is to enable the reader to increase in his desire to please God. *Pleasing God* has invigorated my own faith journey, encouraging me to continue pressing on as I seek ways to honor my Lord and deepen the relationship I have with him. As a reader, you can expect the same! May it be said of us, like with Enoch, that we were pleasing to God.

SUSIE HAWKINS
Women's ministry speaker and author

PREFACE

Hebrews 11:5, which states that Enoch pleased God before his translation to heaven, is one of the most important verses in my life. I have written many books, two of which have similar titles: *Believing God* (based on the people of faith in Hebrews 11) and *Worshipping God* (based on Philippians 3:3—we worship "by the Spirit of God"). However, as I look back on all of these books I am surprised that I have yet to write about this important subject: how to please God.

Pleasing God is a handbook for practical Christian living, a book about how to live a rich Christian life. It is written to reflect on some of my life as pastor at Westminster Chapel from 1977 to 2002 and as an itinerant minister since retiring in 2002. My twenty-five years at Westminster were, to recall the words of Charles Dickens, "the best of times and the worst of times." I fondly remember the greatest compliment I received during my time there, from Ernie Paddon, the church secretary. (In England the church secretary is the major deacon who is right next to the pastor in terms of responsibility and leadership.) He and his wife would often say to me, "You taught us how to live." Ernie was my chief prayer intercessor and committed to pray for me an hour a day—which he did for most of my time at Westminster. He and his wife were stalwart supporters and my greatest encouragers. I dedicate this book to their memory.

This is my second recent book with Thomas Nelson. It has been an honor to work with the legendary Stan Gundry. Dale Williams, my acquisitions editor, has actually become a friend. Emily Voss, who is in charge of publicity, likewise has been a delight to work with. Daniel Saxton, the production editor for this title, has been sharp in offering appropriate suggestions.

I am humbled and grateful that Susie Hawkins has kindly written the foreword to this book. O. S. and Susie have been among the closest friends of my wife and myself for over forty years. My debt to both of them is incalculable. My greatest debt and thanks, however, is to my wife Louise, my best friend and critic.

R. T. KENDALL
Nashville, Tennessee

INTRODUCTION

———— ❧ ————

W hat is this book about? This book is not about God pleasing us. God can do that, of course. Indeed, he loves to do this. But this book has a different focus. Neither does the title of this book intend to convey that God wants us to see how *nice* he is. Some may wish that God exists merely to please us. But the God of the Bible is not like that. Rather, I am gripped by what is written about an ancient man named Enoch. We are not told that God pleased Enoch. No doubt he did. But what we know is that Enoch "pleased God" (Heb. 11:5).

The greatest honor of anyone's lifetime is to have the privilege of pleasing God. But there is more. Why should God *care* whether we please him? For only one reason: he loves us. Why should *we* matter? Because he loves us. To return our love for God by pleasing him is a privilege greater than receiving the Nobel Peace Prize or being honored by Her Majesty Queen Elizabeth II. And yet it is a privilege offered to all of us.

I grew up continually hearing the story I am about to tell you. When my mother was six months pregnant with me, my parents were listening to a sermon in a Nazarene church. My father was so moved by the preaching that he put his hand on my mother's tummy and prayed, "Lord, please let me have a son that will preach like this man."

Nineteen years later I was a student at Trevecca Nazarene College in Nashville, Tennessee, while also serving as a pastor of a Nazarene church in nearby Palmer. I was required to attend chapel every day at Trevecca, which meant I heard hundreds of sermons in my years there. However, I only remember one sermon, from a visiting pastor, C. B. Cox, who took his text from Hebrews 11:5: "By faith Enoch was translated that he should not see death; and was not found, because God had translated him: for before his translation he had this testimony, that he pleased God" (KJV). Pastor Cox dealt with three words: "he pleased God." I was so impacted by that sermon that I rushed to my dormitory room, knelt beside my bed, and earnestly prayed that I could please God like Enoch did.

My father unexpectedly phoned me that same day.

"Today I heard a sermon that touched me very, very deeply," I began, then related some details of the message.

"Who was the preacher?" my dad asked.

"A man by the name of C. B. Cox," I replied.

My dad then said, "Son, that is the very man your mother and I heard when you were still in her womb. I prayed that you might be a preacher like him."

I am convinced that my dad's prayer gave me a head start in wanting to please God. This motivation is why I leaped to embrace John 5:44 when my old mentor, Billy Ball (1927–2015), frequently quoted it to me back in 1956. This verse reads: "How can ye believe, which receive honour one of another, and seek not the honour that cometh from God only?" (KJV). John 5:44 became my "life verse," although I would be a fool if I claim to have lived up to this standard. I have never outgrown the lift I get when people praise me—whether because of a sermon I preached or a book I wrote. And yet I like to believe that this verse enabled me to survive the greatest trials of my life.

I wish I had the anointing that C. B. Cox had when he preached on Hebrews 11:5 at Trevecca many years ago. I remember that he had a calm voice. So many preachers back then shouted when they preached! Not that there is anything wrong with that—I was brought up with shouting preachers in Ashland, Kentucky, as far back as I can remember. Every single one of them shouted. A lot of people in Kentucky and Tennessee in those days felt that unless you shouted when you preached, you weren't preaching. A common example on a preacher's sermon notes during this time was: "weak point, shout here." But I still remember the clear voice of C. B. Cox softly and calmly, stating with extraordinary power: "he pleased God."

I so wish my writing would have a similar effect. I do pray that my book will cause you, the reader, to aspire more than ever *to please God*. I think you would not want to read a book with a title like this if you did not already have a desire to do this.

In the fall of 1955, while I was still at Trevecca, my theology and life unexpectedly changed. I had an extraordinary experience of the Holy Spirit on the morning of Monday, October 31, 1955, while driving from Palmer to Nashville. I saw the face of Jesus. I saw Jesus interceding for me at the right hand of God, making me feel loved in a way I had never felt before. Giving me peace and rest of soul in a way I had never felt before. I had not only inexpressible joy but an assurance that I could never—ever—be lost and that I was chosen. *Not* that I was special. No, nothing like that. But an embryonic understanding of the sovereignty of

God was clearly implanted in my mind and heart by sundown that Monday evening.

Try not to laugh, but I wondered if the Apostle Paul knew about this sort of teaching. I wondered if it was in the Bible! But it did not take long before I saw the New Testament, and the writings of Paul particularly, in an entirely different manner. My belief in the infallibility of Scripture is rooted in that experience.

My chief mentor Dr. Martyn Lloyd-Jones (1899–1981) used to say to me again and again, "Don't forget your Nazarene background." And on the day I was chosen to be the minister of Westminster Chapel, he said to me yet again, "Preach like a Nazarene." I was not sure I understood what Dr. Lloyd-Jones meant because the Nazarenes I knew stressed experience more than biblical knowledge. The reason that he liked me was because I had a combination of Reformed theology and openness to the Holy Spirit.

These things said, this book is not written to change your theology. I want to be used of the Lord to encourage you to have a *desire* solely to please *him*. If this does not happen during your reading of this book, I would be greatly disappointed.

The very idea that God can be pleased—or displeased—shows that he has a mind of his own and a will of his own. He knows exactly what he wants, and we can learn what pleases him. This book has three parts: (1) what pleases God, (2) why we should please God, and (3) how we should please God. It is not primarily about how to be saved. It is about pleasing God after one has been saved.

Pleasing God is not an uphill climb. It is the most delightful and delectable venture imaginable this side of heaven. My prayer is that you will experience this—*feel* this—from this moment.

PART I

WHAT PLEASES GOD?

CHAPTER 1

GOOD WORKS

❧

For by grace you have been saved through faith. And this is not your own doing; it is the gift of God, not a result of works, so that no one may boast. For we are his workmanship, created in Christ Jesus for good works, which God prepared beforehand, that we should walk in them.
—EPHESIANS 2:8–10

God does not need your good works, but your neighbor does.
—MARTIN LUTHER (1483–1546)

It may surprise you, if you know anything about me, that I would challenge you to please God. The very notion of pleasing God brings up the idea of earning one's salvation. And I would never tell people that they could ever do anything to make God owe them salvation. Salvation is a free gift. However, in the introduction to this book I said that Scripture tells us to please God. And we know from the book of Hebrews that Enoch pleased God.

In order to teach you about pleasing God, I need to talk about good works and Enoch.

There is good news and bad news. The good news is time in prayer and practicing total forgiveness are not requirements for being born again, nor are these conditions for remaining saved. Once saved, always saved. Total forgiveness is indeed a very good "work."

If you are not familiar with my writing and speaking, let me briefly tell you what I mean when I say "total forgiveness." Total forgiveness is the idea that you totally let your enemy—any person who hurt you—completely off the hook. You commit to truly praying for them to be blessed by God. To me this is a good work because it is the hardest thing in the world to do.

Time in prayer is also a good work. But we are not saved by works, or even the best of works. Rather, we are saved by the sheer grace of God. Indeed, salvation is not of works, lest we boast (Eph. 2:8–9)! God is determined to save us in such a manner so that there will be no boasting before him (1 Cor. 1:29). Be thankful for this; otherwise, neither you nor I nor anybody else would ever be saved. The standard God requires to get into heaven is so high that nobody ever comes up to it. Entrance into glory requires total perfection sixty seconds a minute, sixty minutes an hour, twenty-four hours a day, three hundred sixty-five days a year, and three hundred sixty-six days when it is a leap year. Only Jesus met the standard; he never—ever—sinned. He lived a perfect life for us. He kept the Law for us—indeed, keeping all 613 pieces of Mosaic legislation. Jesus was even baptized for us. The reason he was baptized was *not for himself but for us*—to "fulfill all righteousness" (Matt. 3:15). Only Jesus consistently practiced total forgiveness; he alone was "without sin" (Heb. 4:15).

You and I are saved when we are truly sorry for our sins, transfer our trust in our good works to the blood Jesus shed on the cross, and give our lives to the Lord Jesus Christ as best as we know how. We are justified (made righteous in God's sight) by faith alone in Christ alone. It is, as Francis Schaeffer (1912–1984) so often put it, "Faith plus nothing." The faithful Bible reader that you are might ask me, "R. T., how should we understand Jesus's words from Matthew 6:15, 'If you do not forgive others their trespasses, neither will your Father forgive your trespasses'?" That verse must be taken in its context. This is from the Sermon on the Mount, in which Jesus is showing how we inherit God's kingdom, namely, by dwelling in the realm of the ungrieved Spirit. (I will talk more about how we inherit the kingdom and abide with the ungrieved Spirit in chapters 5 and 10.) As I show in detail in my book *The Sermon on the Mount*, the Sermon on the Mount is Jesus's doctrine of the Holy Spirit. Its main focus is how to exceed the righteousness of the religious Pharisees through fellowship with God, intimacy with him, and pleasing him. The Sermon on the Mount is not telling us how to be saved; it applies to those already saved.

Good works are to be demonstrated to others—not to assure ourselves that we are saved. Instead, we get our assurance by looking directly to Christ—not to ourselves. If we look to ourselves, that is "sure damnation," warned John Calvin (1509–1564). James stresses works in chapter 2 of his letter, and good works are for others—not for a person's personal assurance of salvation. James does not tell a person, "Get your assurance by works." Rather, he has the person in mind who struggles to believe our gospel because that person does not see Jesus in us. James urges Christians (probably Jews in Jerusalem) not to show favoritism to the rich person but to the "poor man" who comes to their assembly (James 2:1ff). Indeed, he rebukes them: you have "dishonored the poor man" (Gr. *ptochon*, v. 6). Traditional interpreters seem to have overlooked the fact that James never once changes the subject throughout chapter 2—all the way to its end! So, when James says, "Can that faith save *him*?" (Gr. *auton*, v. 14, emphasis mine), he is still talking about the poor man referred to in verse 6. The question, then, is, "Can that faith save the poor man?" No! Rather, that poor man needs to see our good works!

This shows there is not the slightest difference of theology between James and Paul. I deal with James 2:14 in my volume on James entitled *Justification by Works* and also in *Whatever Happened to the Gospel?* Some will be interested to know that when Dr. Martyn Lloyd-Jones heard my treatment of James 2:14, he said, "You have convinced me." I also shared my thoughts with Dr. W. A. Criswell when he visited us in London, and he was equally pleased with my understanding of this verse. The rest of James 2 reads by itself, with no need to bend a verse. Although Martin Luther was not happy with James, he should have applied his own statement, "God does not need your good works, but your neighbor does," to it!

Now for the sobering news: we cannot please God after we are saved if we consciously do the things that displease him. This includes the area of total forgiveness. For instance, Jesus said that if we don't forgive, we commit murder (Matt. 5:21–22, 43ff). And if we lust, we commit adultery (vv. 27–29). Paul also said that "love is the fulfilling of the law" (Rom. 13:10). This is carried out by exceeding the righteousness of the Pharisees (Matt. 5:20). The Pharisees were widely regarded as the most righteous and most religious people on earth. But, according to their own interpretation of the Law, it appears they could hate people—withhold forgiveness—and remain good Pharisees. So long as Pharisees kept their hands to themselves and did not act on immoral desires—commit adultery or look lustfully at women—they considered themselves as good Pharisees. However, Jesus's teaching in the Sermon on the Mount tells us that this type of outward righteousness isn't enough.

How could we surpass the righteousness of the Pharisees? Don't think that because you are not a Pharisee that you don't live similarly. My own observation has been that the chief sin of preachers today is pornography. For our righteousness to exceed that of the Pharisees we need to do more than keep up outward appearances. Here are two practical examples: (1) totally forgive people that have done you wrong—that is, sincerely ask God to bless them; and (2) refuse to indulge in lust by objectifying people as sexual objects. Rather, choose to look at men and women with respect because, like you, they are made in the image of God.

According to Paul, to love—demonstrated by carrying out Jesus's spiritual interpretation of the Ten Commandments—is fulfilling the law. The righteousness that exceeds that of the Pharisees is not external but internal righteousness—what is in our hearts. This means that we must indeed forgive "from [the] heart" (Matt. 18:35) and "make no provision for the flesh, to gratify its desires" (Rom. 13:14)—a righteousness alien to the legalistic views of the Pharisees. In short, pleasing God is a goal carried out by our internal desire, not merely external righteousness.

TWO KINDS OF FAITH

There are two kinds of faith: saving faith and persistent faith.

Saving faith is the faith that comes alive when you hear the gospel. It is what I referred to earlier: transferring your hope in good works to the blood of Jesus.

Persistent faith is what we are required to live by once we have been saved. Faith itself—whether saving faith or persevering faith (as some might prefer to call it)—is defined and translated in Hebrews 11:1 variously as the substance—assurance, certainty—of things hoped for, the evidence of things not seen.

This book aims to unfold what persistent faith is and what it does for both us and God. Persistent faith *follows* saving faith. It means you do not give up. It is not merely believing that God "exists" but that you persevere, trusting in God's rewarding of your diligence in seeking him (v. 6).

The natural man says, "I will believe it only when I see it." But according to Hebrews 11:1, you cannot call it *faith* if you see it. Rather, it is faith when you don't see but still believe. For instance, we believe the Bible without any tangible, empirical evidence that it is true. The secular atheist says, "That's insane." But this is part of the cross we bear when we accept the offense—the embarrassment or shame—that goes with being a Christian. We are often required to look like fools!

Hebrews 11 describes people who changed their world by persevering faith. I wish all who have saving faith automatically had persevering faith like the saints of Hebrews 11 by consistently pleasing God and continually doing great things, never backsliding. But according to 1 Corinthians 3:11–15, fire will reveal the truth about a saved person's life; some will experience the horror of their works being burned on the "Day" (v. 13). Nevertheless, they will be saved by fire and granted entrance into heaven because they were on the foundation—Jesus Christ (v. 11). Martin Luther once said that he expects three surprises when he is in heaven: there will be those present whom he did not expect to be there; there will be those missing whom he thought would be there; and that he is there himself! I think Luther was being intentionally humorous about the third surprise, although Dr. Lloyd-Jones used to say that a true Christian is surprised to be a Christian. He added that if one is not surprised to be a Christian, he wondered if this person has been truly converted!

Hebrews 11 shows what persevering faith can do; it describes those who truly pleased God by their persistence. They turned their world upside down by *believing God*. That was Dr. Lloyd-Jones's definition of faith: believing God. Those referred to in Hebrews 11:4–40 were required to do unprecedented things. Noah walked with God (Gen. 6:9). Yet he was not taken to heaven (as he might have wished) but was required to build an ark (Heb. 11:7). Abraham was actually called a friend of God (Isa. 41:8; James 2:23), but he still had to obey God's call to leave his homeland without knowing where he was going (Heb. 11:8)! However, Enoch walked with God (Gen. 5:22) and was translated to heaven without dying. Not a single person in Hebrews 11 had the luxury of repeating what had been done before.

Do you want to please God? If so, are you willing to do what no one has been required to do before?

ENOCH

All that Enoch did in his lifetime could be summed up in these words: he "pleased God." That was his main accomplishment. This is the greatest thing that can be said about a human being. Enoch did other things too; he was a prophet. This means he heard from

God. Jude says that Enoch prophesied about the second coming of Jesus thousands of years ago: "Behold, the Lord comes with ten thousands of his holy ones" (Jude 14).

If a person achieved a thousand Nobel Prizes, was regarded as the greatest leader of his or her nation, or was said to do more good for the poor than Mother Teresa, all this still falls short of the honor to have pleased God. It does not get any better than this!

Pleasing God is an achievement greater than any other accomplishment that can be conceived. The feeling of having pleased God as you near the end of your life is sweeter than anything else that can be imagined.

Enoch had the "testimony"—the witness—that he pleased God. It was the witness of the Holy Spirit. He was not commended by people, by friends, or by enemies. Jesus similarly lived by faith while on this earth (Heb. 2:13; Isa. 8:17), saying that he always did what pleases the Father (John 8:29). He had the witness from heaven that he pleased the Father when he was baptized by John the Baptist (Matt. 3:17). This witness was repeated when Jesus was transfigured on the mountain (17:5). It is what Paul meant by Jesus being vindicated by the Spirit (1 Tim. 3:16).

God gave this satisfaction to Enoch, who knew that he pleased God. God will also do this for you and me. We may not be translated to heaven in advance of the second coming, but God would not have given us the command, "Find out what pleases the Lord" (Eph. 5:10 NIV), if it were out of reach. God is not like that; his commands are not demoralizing. Finding true wisdom may cost you "all you have" (Prov. 4:7 NIV), yes, but the cost is not unreasonable—and is worth it. Prize this wisdom "highly," said Solomon. "She will exalt you; she will honor you if you embrace her. She will place on your head a graceful garland; she will bestow on you a beautiful crown" (vv. 8–9).

The cost is related to our ego, which promotes such vices as pride, self-esteem, and wanting to please people rather than God. What can never—ever—be underestimated is the relationship of our pride to the glory of God. Get ready for this truth, if it should surprise you: God is jealous. This is no joke; God is no respecter of persons. If pride causes one to resent God's jealousy, so be it: God will not bend to you or me in order to compromise his essential nature. That said, his jealousy is for our good. The more you get to know God, the more you will cherish him for being exactly as he is.

The writer of Hebrews does not tell us all that Enoch specifically did which pleased God. We only know that he walked with God and that he heard from God. For example, the writer does not say that Enoch pleased his parents. That can sometimes be hard to do. My first report card when I was six years old and a student in Crabbe Elementary School in Ashland, Kentucky, had 3 Bs and 3 Cs. I remember being sobered by this, knowing that it would not thrill my dad. He said, "Son, work harder and you will bring those grades up to all Bs." I did. After that, my father raised the bar: "Work hard, and you will have all Bs and some As." I did. Later my dad challenged, "Work really hard, and you will have all As." I did—but some were A minuses. And what do you suppose my dad noticed first?

My dad meant well. I regard him as a good father and a godly man—indeed, the most godly man I ever knew. My first memory of him was seeing him on his knees in prayer for thirty minutes every morning. His praying for me when I was in my mother's womb—as I said earlier—is why I had a head start in living the

Christian life. His example of praying is why I began praying daily as a teenager. But my dad was not perfect. I do think some of my struggles with the feeling that I do not please God is because I was not always sure I pleased my dad. Therefore, I have had to rise above my upbringing to reach the place where I was pleasing God.

Here is more good news: you don't have to be perfect and without sin to please God. My Nazarene background, added to my father's strict demands, did not help me many years ago. Some of the main leaders—not all, but some—taught sinless perfection. What set me free long ago and sets me free now is 1 John 1:8: "If we *say* we have no sin, we deceive ourselves, and the truth is not in us" (emphasis mine). If perfection were possible in this life, Jesus would not have given us the petition in the Lord's Prayer, "Forgive us our debts [trespasses or sins]" (Matt. 6:12; Luke 11:4).

If you had a parent or an authority figure in your childhood who was overly strict and unreasonable, it is not unlikely that you struggle with the thought of pleasing God. Thankfully, God himself understands this! A possible quick shortcut to overcoming this is embracing John 14:9—the very words of Jesus—"Whoever has seen me has seen the Father." Look to Jesus. He was—and is—the perfect combination of truth and grace, and of justice and compassion. He puts us in our place with tenderness. He is our intercessor day and night, having never forgotten what it was like to be tempted at every level when he walked on this planet (Heb. 4:15).

Furthermore, the word concerning Enoch does not say that he pleased his friends. You have heard the expression, "With a friend like that, who needs an enemy?" Some of my best friends—including those I admired most—have been the most hurtful to me. I have thought of writing a book called *When Relationships Turn Sour.*

Hebrews 11:5 also does not say that Enoch pleased his authority figures or mentors (assuming he had such). I have lived long enough to observe that *every person I began to admire a little bit too much sooner or later disappointed me.* This is not their fault; it is mine. I should never put any human being on a pedestal. I have almost certainly hurt people, although not intentionally. If you got to know me very well, I would eventually disappoint you! So, too, would those you admire too much. It is only a matter of time before we see unpleasant weaknesses in the best of people. The best of men are men at best. I doubt you would enjoy a long holiday with Elijah, Peter, or Paul. Only Jesus was perfect. And yet even he disappointed Mary and Martha (John 11:21, 32), showing that our flawed expectations don't always line up with what God does. I have actually written a book, *Totally Forgiving God* (criticized for the title rather than the contents), grappling with why God allows things he could have stopped—whether COVID-19, tornadoes, or untimely deaths of loved ones. God the Father is the most maligned person in the entire universe. He is cursed countless times daily but waits for the day when he will explain things.

Additionally, Hebrews 11:5 is silent about if Enoch pleased his wife. Sometimes that is hard to do!

A man once came to me after a sermon in Northern Ireland with this question: "Can your wife be your enemy?"

I looked at him, then paused and said, "Yes."

"Thank you," he replied.

The man went on to express gratitude for a book he thought I wrote called *Unhappy Marriage.* I told him that I had not written a book with this title.

"Oh, yes, you have—it changed my life," he insisted.

Then I remembered that my book *The Thorn in the Flesh* has a chapter entitled "Unhappy Marriage." That, to him, was the book!

Louise and I sought marriage counseling for several weeks during our years in London. (I refer to this in my book *In Pursuit of His Glory*.) There are always exceptions, but most marriages sooner or later could benefit from a third party—if qualified—helping them work through issues that are often ignored. But our problem is often that we are too proud to admit we need help!

The writer of Hebrews did not say that Enoch pleased his enemies. You may be sure he had them. When Jesus commanded us to love our enemies, he assumed we would have them. He told us to pray, "Forgive us our debts, as we also have forgiven our debtors" (Matt. 6:12), because we all have those whom we must forgive. I needed this teaching during our most difficult days in Westminster. I have had a number of books written against me, as well as countless articles. One man (now in heaven) took notes during my sermons in hopes of snagging quotes he could use to attack me in his next book! But this was still good for me. I think God raises up adversaries partly to keep us on our toes!

I actually have an enemies' prayer list (I'm not joking). It was hard at first to pray for my enemies (and ask God sincerely to bless them), but over time it not only became easy but was an incalculable blessing. I would urge you to pray sincerely for your enemies. You don't pray for them merely for a day or two; you do it daily until the day you die. Don't despise the person God has picked for your sanctification. Moreover, that very person may one day be your good friend!

We are not told that Enoch pleased himself. Indeed, even Christ did not please himself (Rom. 15:3). He did not come to do his own will but the will of the Father (John 5:30). Christ is

your model. You are not your own; you are bought with a price
(1 Cor. 6:19–20).

And, as I said earlier, we are not told that God pleased Enoch.
Nevertheless, you can be sure that God did please Enoch—I do
not doubt this. That said, and I don't mean to be unkind, but I fear
many leaders only portray a God who is a God all people will like.
These leaders seem to extol a God who will do whatever *we* want
him to do—he exists only to make us feel good, to prosper us, to
heal us, and to make us happy. They say that if anything adverse
happens to any of us, it is from the devil—not God. Or it might be
from our lack of faith. Such leaders either do not know their Bibles
or refuse to believe their Bibles! It displeases God when we pick
and choose from his Word. If we truly love him and want to please
him, we will embrace *all of his Word*. We do know that God granted
Israel's ill-posed request for special food in the wilderness—"he
gave them what they asked, but sent a wasting disease among
them" (Ps. 106:15). God did this because the people of Israel followed their fleshly desires when they asked him for something.
They bypassed the truth that God has a will of his own, so he had
to discipline them. Likewise, if we don't respect his will—what *he*
has determined is good and right—we are fools. Fools.

So, God knows what is best for us. He will not withhold any
good thing from those who want to please him (Ps. 84:11).

Here is what we know about Enoch: he pleased God.

You and I must make a choice: who do you want to please? The
irony is, if you try to please people you will fail both ways. First,
sadly, you won't please anyone indefinitely. Second, sadly, you forfeit pleasing God. I urge you: set your goal to please God. Nothing
else matters at the end of the day. The pain in the meantime—and
the cost to your pride—is worth it all.

A SUGGESTION TO YOU

Consider this question: which gives you more satisfaction—when God is pleasing you or when you are pleasing him? I will try to be fair. Of course we prefer it when God pleases us—when he answers prayer, gives us joy, heals our bodies, prospers us, provides us with friends who are well connected, and opens doors for us. But I issue this challenge: seek to get your joy from pleasing God, not from when he pleases you! I confess that I find it hard to practice what I preach when it comes to this topic. It just so happens that during the time of my writing this section—at this very moment—Louise and I are in our greatest trial in years. Right now are almost certainly the worst days of our lives. During this time I have kept praying, "Lord, please step in." It is *as though* the Lord is saying, "You preach that people should get their satisfaction by pleasing me. Now you practice what you preach." I cannot testify that I have been very good at doing this, but I do know this: there is immense, deep, and thrilling satisfaction from knowing you are pleasing God in your testing.

The Lord never said pleasing him would be effortless. As C. S. Lewis put it, concerning Aslan the lion: "I never said he is safe. But he's good." Thus, I do not say it is always easy to please God. But it is satisfying.

CHAPTER 2

FAITHFULNESS THAT PLEASES GOD

———— ❧ ————

By faith Enoch was taken up so that he should not see death,
and he was not found, because God had taken him. Now
before he was taken he was commended as having pleased
God. And without faith it is impossible to please him, for
whoever would draw near to God must believe that he exists
and that he rewards those who seek him.
—HEBREWS 11:5–6

You can't go back and change the beginning, but you can
start where you are and change the ending.
—C. S. LEWIS (1898–1963)

W HEN I succeeded Dr. Martyn Lloyd-Jones in Westminster
Chapel, he had great hopes for me. After I had been the
minister there for a few months, he enthusiastically predicted to
me, "You are going to do what I did." Dr. Lloyd-Jones was referring

to the size of the congregation, which had grown during his time. But I never achieved that. He also predicted that a fresh filling of the Spirit would come on me.

"When will this come?" I asked.

"Anytime," he replied.

One afternoon while I was spending time with Dr. Lloyd-Jones, he asked me to kneel. He then laid his hands on me and prayed for me. "Don't do anything that displeases the Lord," he advised.

I remember asking, "Is *not displeasing* him the same as *pleasing* him?"

"Yes," he answered.

For some reason I needed to hear this.

Those words keep ringing in my ears: "Don't do anything that displeases the Lord."

"Find out what pleases the Lord," Paul advised (Eph. 5:10 NIV). In Galatians he put it like this: "For am I now seeking the approval of man, or of God? Or am I trying to please man? If I were still trying to please man, I would not be a servant of Christ" (Gal. 1:10). Rather, we should walk "to please God" (1 Thess. 4:1). Indeed, we need to do what is "fully pleasing to him" (Col. 1:10).

I understand Paul saying that to please God is a lifetime process. This is a process that you, dear reader, must begin now. I promise you that the more you read and know your Bible, plus the more time you spend alone in prayer, you will find out what pleases the Lord—and also what displeases him.

Part I has been the easiest part of this book to write: *what it is* that pleases God. I am reminded of what Charles Spurgeon (1834–1892), possibly the greatest preacher of all time, said about the school he founded—the School of the Prophets. Spurgeon remarked that he could not teach a person *how* to preach, but he could certainly teach one *what* to preach. In other words, he might not create another Spurgeon, but he could convey *what* he believed and preached. Likewise, I find it relatively easy to state *what* pleases God—it is not hard to find.

If you and I go by what the Bible teaches, it is fairly easy to deduce what pleases God.

Later in this book, I will endeavor to show how to please God. I may possibly get it right in writing *how* to please God. But at some point you, the reader, are on your own—to discover for yourself what grips you and what compels you to want to please God. We all have our strengths and weaknesses, our likes and dislikes, and things that appeal to us as well as things that don't. For instance, I use the Robert Murray M'Cheyne Bible reading plan; Louise sticks to a plan she has used for years. When we go out to eat, I prefer the starters; Louise prefers desserts. I like salty things; she likes sweets. I like steaks rare; she likes them well done. I like dressings on salads; she could do without any dressing on them (which always amazes me!).

If you have a desire to please God, thank him for this. If your desire to please him is strong, burning, and earnest, be very, very thankful. Only God could put a desire like that in your heart—that desire did not come from the flesh. Satan didn't produce it. The Holy Spirit put that desire there, and he would not mock you with this aspiration. It means you will have the knowledge—the witness that you are pleasing him—in ever-increasing measure. Congratulations. "He will give you the desires of your heart" (Ps. 37:4).

Over fifty years ago I had lunch with the legendary Richard Wurmbrand (1909–2001). I felt so honored. He became famous when he testified before the U. S. Senate, took off his shirt before senators and cameras, and showed his bare wounds and scars from his physical torture in Romania by the Communists. He also wrote the book *Tortured for Christ*, where he described his fourteen years' imprisonment.

I asked Wurmbrand for any bit of wisdom he might give me. He instantly replied: "Young man, spend more time talking to God about men than talking to men about God." No one had ever said anything like that to me—before or since. I remember it as though it were yesterday.

After I moved back to America from London, a pastor asked me, "What has a veteran like you got to say to a young whipper-snapper like me?" I paused for a second, and then replied: "Find out what grieves the Holy Spirit *and don't do that.*"

It is so easy to grieve the Spirit. This is mainly done by anger or holding a grudge. As soon as Paul said, "Do not grieve the Holy Spirit of God, by whom you were sealed for the day of redemption," he immediately continued, "Let all bitterness and wrath and anger and clamor and slander be put away from you, along with all malice. Be kind to one another, tenderhearted, forgiving one another, as God in Christ forgave you" (Eph. 4:30–32). Paul added these words because of our proneness to snap back or say something unkind at someone. Many of us tend to speak against others without letting this bother us. But it is only a matter of time before we will be forced to see that the little foxes often spoil the vines (Song 2:15). Sweeping excuses for our anger under the carpet only postpones our ability to see how we can displease the Lord. "He that is faithful in that which is least is faithful also in much: and he that is unjust in the least is unjust also in much" (Luke 16:10 KJV).

The more time you spend alone with God, the more sensitive you will be to things that displease him. Therefore, when you resolve to find out what *displeases him—and don't do these things*, you have your work cut out for you! As I said, the chief way we tend to grieve the Spirit is by bitterness. Paul culminated this important admonition by expressing the need for total forgiveness. In light of this, I am ashamed to say that for years—too many years—I swept the need to forgive people under the carpet. I knew I was saved, but I dismissed the idea of having to forgive people who hurt me. "Nobody's perfect," I said to myself, refusing to acknowledge that anger and the holding of a grudge bothered me. I lived in denial. Finally, one day—during the deepest hurt of my life—Josif Ton of Romania said to me, "R. T., you must totally forgive them. Until you totally forgive them, you will be in chains. Release them, and you will be released."

Isn't that interesting? Two Romanians gave me life-changing words. Josif Ton was a protégé of Richard Wurmbrand. As Martyn Lloyd-Jones was my mentor, Richard Wurmbrand was Josif's mentor.

Spending more time talking to God about men than talking to men about God will not make you perfect. Ironically, it will enable you to see your sinfulness and unworthiness more than ever! But this combination will make it easier to discern what is pleasing to God.

TWELVE PRINCIPLES THAT PLEASE GOD

Let's briefly examine twelve principles of *what pleases God*. What follows are twelve biblical teachings especially needed today. They will help you understand what pleases God in general. I start at God's eternal existence before creation and conclude with the final judgment. "For the LORD gives wisdom; from his mouth come knowledge and understanding" (Prov. 2:6). I believe this theology pleases God.

I. GOD'S PRIVILEGE AND PURPOSE

"Our God is in the heavens; he does all that he pleases" (Ps. 115:3). "Whatever the LORD pleases, he does, in heaven and on earth, in the seas and all deeps" (135:6). God "is" (Heb. 11:6 KJV)—that is, he "exists" (ESV). This means God is *there*—whether we like it or not. Or whether we like him or not. I urge that all readers salute God for being there and also for being like who he is. We must affirm him and freely acknowledge his privilege of being God. All of us by nature—our sinful nature, that is—resent God; Jonathan Edwards believed that God and his fallen creation are mutual enemies. Human beings after the fall hate God. We may not hate the god we might *wish* him to be, but the God revealed in Holy Scripture—a "God of glory" (Acts 7:2), a jealous God whose very *name* is "Jealous" (Ex. 34:14)—is the God we hate. Satan is incapable of producing in us an unfeigned love for the God of the Bible. Therefore, when we *love* the God who is revealed in Scripture, it is an infallible sign that the true God has done a gracious work in us. We must never forget that God did not make himself like he is; he did not create himself. God is the way he is and was and is to come. He is unchangeable (Mal. 3:6).

"Of his own will," said James, God "brought us forth by the word of truth" (James 1:18). He who is "the Alpha and Omega . . . who is and who was and who is to come, the Almighty" (Rev. 1:8), made a decision before there was anything in existence but the triune God. Call it what happened in eternity before there was ever a star, a blade of grass, or a speck of dust; when there was nothing but God. There was no rival, no competition. There was no one else to consult. There were no angels—good or bad. There was only God Almighty—the Father; the Word, who was with God, who was God, and who became flesh (John 1:1, 14); and the Spirit.

This God is the God of the Bible. The God who is described in the Bible. The God who lovingly reached out to a sinful world. The God who has a will and a mind of his own. A God which nobody can conceive a greater being than. The God who chose to have a people, a people which "no one could number" (Rev. 7:9). You and I are in that number. We have discovered that he is a jealous God, and we should see clearly forever and ever that he is not going to surrender his sovereignty or the privilege of being God. Anyone who begins to have a glimpse of this God will be in awe. When believers embrace all these truths about God, he is pleased.

2. CREATION

When God created the universe and all he had made, he saw that "it was very good" (Gen. 1:31). That means God was pleased with his creation. "By faith we understand that the universe was created by the word of God, so that what is seen was not made out of things that are visible" (Heb. 11:3). This is known as creation *ex nihilo*; God created the universe out of nothing but his word. He merely said, "Let there be light," and there was light (Gen. 1:3). Creation was a trinitarian operation; God said, "Let us make man in our image, after our likeness" (v. 26). "The Spirit of God was hovering over the face of the waters" (v. 2) and the eternal Word was equally our Creator (John 1:3): "by him all things were created, in heaven and on earth, visible and invisible, whether thrones or dominions or rulers or authorities—all things were created through him and for him. And he is before all things, and in him all things hold together" (Col. 1:16–17).

Creation was God's idea; he did not have to create. What is seen—what is there—was not always there and was not created out of what is there. This means that *matter is not eternal.* The existence of matter was put there by God the Creator. We must never forget this.

I do not plan to go deeply into the subject of evolution. Believing chapter one of Genesis, I only know that we are to understand that creation came "out of nothing." Hebrews 11:3 tells us, "By faith we understand that the universe was created by the word of God, so that what is seen was not made out of things that are visible." Influential scientists and philosophers have tried to explain earth's origins in various ways because they will not accept what Hebrews 11:3 plainly states. Placing our faith in the teaching of Scripture that God created the world without help or from any preexisting matter is a principle that brings pleasure to God. To summarize: our challenge and mandate is to believe in creation *ex nihilo*—"out of nothing."

3. THE IMAGE OF GOD

He created humankind in his own image: "male and female he created them" (Gen. 1:27). I do not fully understand the implications of Genesis 1:27. What is clear is that God wanted humankind to be male and female and "said to them, 'Be fruitful and multiply and fill the earth and subdue it'" (v. 28).

Therefore, when we talk about choosing what sex we want to be, we are in that moment repudiating God himself. God not only created man and woman in the garden of Eden; he decided *who* would be born, *when* we would be born, and *where* we would be born (Acts 17:26). God was pleased when David said, "You knitted me together in my mother's womb. I praise you, for I am fearfully and wonderfully made. Wonderful are your works; my soul knows it very well" (Ps. 139:13–14).

I used to get my haircut from a unisex salon in England. I didn't think much about it then—this was over forty years ago. But since then I have realized that this salon was a symptom of a society that is more and more anti-God. Consciously or unconsciously in defiance against the God of the Bible, the world wants to avoid any distinction between male and female, blurring their differences. This may be seen not only in hairstyles but in clothes, appearance, sports, natural abilities, or jobs. Men who get a sex change are now competing with and outperforming women in sports such as swimming and tennis. I do not say that people who get a sex change are consciously defying God, but one who believes in the God of the Bible would not opt for such an operation.

The issue of the image of God is at the heart of the rebellion of humanity today. These people rarely believe in God and do not necessarily consciously hate him, but nonetheless they are determined to overthrow what Christians historically stood for—things that were once thought to be of God. They want to be rid of anything that smacks of traditional values. Satan is behind this entire movement to destroy morality, marriage, and the family. We are thus living in a time when Christians need to be reminded of the truth that we are all created in God's image. Reiterating this important truth pleases God. The doctrine of the image of God is extensive, including such topics as human identity, race, coequality, creativity, knowledge, work, and serving one another in love. This also means racism must be eschewed. All human beings in the world have the image of God in them; therefore, God is displeased when we treat fellow men and women with prejudice and indignity.

4. MARRIAGE

From the revelation of God's image in Genesis 1:27 followed his will regarding marriage: "Therefore a man shall leave his father and his mother and hold fast to his wife, and they shall become one flesh" (2:24). This was God's ordaining sexual intercourse between a man and woman; he intended that they should marry in order to populate the earth. Thus, marriage being a heterosexual union was not open to question. Indeed, Genesis 2:24 is often written into the marriage vows of Christian weddings.

Marriage was not only to be heterosexual but monogamous and permanent. God could have continued creating every human being one at a time—each man out of dust and each woman with a man's rib. He could have let every person be born as Adam and Eve were before the Fall—*posse peccare* (able to sin)—indefinitely. However, it was God's will to create Adam and Eve—our first parents—in the garden of Eden and then give the command: "Be fruitful and multiply and fill the earth and subdue it" (1:28). He intended this pattern to endure.

Consequently, God has always condemned homosexual practice, from the time of Moses to the apostolic era. Moses said that a man should not lie with a man as with a woman; such is an "abomination" (Lev. 18:22; 20:13). Paul also equally condemned "men who practice homosexuality" (1 Cor. 6:9). No one for centuries seriously questioned where the Bible stood in this matter. But same-sex practice crossed over a line that had been unthinkable only a short while ago when the legalizing of same-sex unions occurred and the demand came for same-sex marriage. Thus, due to the rising number of people engaging in homosexual practice alongside the falling number of Christians who would stand up and be counted for biblical truth, same-sex marriage became accepted and legal almost overnight. This slap in the face of God's own image is now embedded in normal life. Even ministers who had been historically evangelical are now marrying same-sex couples right, left, and center.

Paul refers to "nature" teaching us (11:14). Even animals are male and female. Even people in countries where the gospel has never entered—or been prominent—have overwhelmingly disdained homosexual practice. However, those countries in which the gospel had once been respected—like England and America—have sadly taken the lead in championing gay marriage. This is symptomatic of the apostate faith in nations once generally unashamed of Jesus Christ.

A marriage that pleases God will affirm that God created humankind male and female. It will be heterosexual, monogamous, and permanent. I once wrote a book called *Is God for the Homosexual?* My answer to this book's title is "Yes." My heart does go out to all people grappling with same-sex attraction. God loves them. Jesus loves them. All Christians should love them and sympathize with them. We must equally love and sympathize with any single person, especially those who desperately do not like being single. Jesus understands and loves them; he is deeply concerned for our feelings (Heb. 4:15). But the same Jesus also commands all—whatever their sexual proclivity—to abandon a life of sin (John 8:11). Please never forget that Jesus never apologized for the God of the Old Testament, who made it clear in the

Mosaic law that homosexual practice is sin (e.g., Lev. 18:22; 20:13). The God of the Old and New Testaments is the same.

5. SIN

We need to (1) recognize the truth about the fall and the origin of sin; (2) see the essential work of the Holy Spirit in people being saved; and (3) acknowledge the importance of the awareness of sin in believers. God is pleased when we affirm the difficult truth of what happened in the garden of Eden. I do believe that the garden of Eden was a place on the map and that the fall of humankind was a date in history.

St. Augustine (354–430) famously said that humankind should be envisaged in four stages: (1) God created humankind *posse peccare* (able to sin; Gen. 2:15–17). After Adam and Eve sinned, the result was death—(2) *non posse non peccare* (not able not to sin). But when God rescued humankind and initially signified redemption by preparing animal skins for Adam and Eve, humankind was (3) *posse non peccare* (able not to sin). Finally, the day will come when humankind is glorified (Rom. 8:30) and thus rendered (4) *non posse peccare* (not able to sin).

Affirming the doctrine of sin is vital: Jesus said that the Holy Spirit will initially convict the world of sin (John 16:8). When Isaiah saw the glory of God, he also saw his own sin (Isa. 6:5). And the Apostle John said, "If we say we have no sin, we deceive ourselves, and the truth is not in us" (1 John 1:8).

Have you ever wondered what keeps the world from being topsy-turvy and worse than it is? God's common grace does this; John Calvin called it "special grace in nature." Common grace refers to God's goodness to everyone, giving us hospitals, medicine, policemen, firemen, schools, etc. Our gifts, intelligence, educational structures, scientific advancements, and laws are also given by God's kindness. He makes the rain fall and the sun rise on the just and the unjust (Matt. 5:45). Common grace comes to all—whether or not they are saved. Although all people experience this blessing—whether rich or poor, famous or brilliant—they still need to see their sin. They need to hear the effectual calling of the Spirit that comes only through the preaching of the gospel.

Why is the subject of sin important? First, many want to deny that sin exists. Some want to emphasize human potential and goodness while closing their eyes to evil, increasing crime, and injustice. Second, when we are able to see our own sin—accusing ourselves rather than blaming others—this shows God is pleased with us. I suggest we pray this daily: that God will show us both our sin and the next step we can take forward to bring him honor and glory in our lives.

6. JUSTICE OF GOD

God is a God of *fairness*—we can be so thankful for this. His justice may be administered in wrath, or it may be shown in mercy. Either way, it will be absolutely right. Paul believed in this truth so much that he said to the Corinthians, God "will bring to light the things now hidden in darkness and will disclose the purposes of the heart. Then each one will receive his commendation from God" (1 Cor. 4:5).

The father of faith, Abraham, knew this about God. Although he did not understand why God would judge Sodom and Gomorrah without warning them, he said, "Shall not the Judge of all the earth do what is just?" (Gen. 18:25). Bethan, the wife of Martyn Lloyd-Jones, used to share with me how she leaned on that verse when it came to the subject of eternal punishment in hell.

As to why God allows evil in the world to continue when he could stop it at any moment, the answer is—at least partly—so that we might have faith. God decreed that people would affirm him by faith, which is believing without seeing the evidence (Heb. 11:1). If there were no evil, there would be no need for faith.

There are some things that God does not want us to understand. The burning bush, for example, perplexed Moses. (It would cause you distress, too!) A bush ablaze that did not burn up got Moses's attention. As he approached the bush, God said in so many words, "STOP. Don't come any closer" (Ex. 3:5). God only let Moses get so close, then told him to take off his shoes and worship. Why? God chooses to keep some things to himself. What pleases him is when we take off our shoes and worship by affirming him for being who he is.

The prophet Habakkuk wanted to know why God allowed evil, unfairness, and injustice while he turned his back on his own people without explaining why. In response, God taught Habakkuk a lesson: that the answer will come at the *end* (Hab. 2:3)—namely, the final judgment. Furthermore, God told him that the just will live by the faithfulness of God (v. 4). Habakkuk might have shaken his fist at God and said, "That's not good enough." But he accepted God's verdict and said,

> Though the fig tree should not blossom,
> nor fruit be on the vines,
> the produce of the olive fail
> and the fields yield no food,
> the flock be cut off from the fold
> and there be no herd in the stalls,

yet I will rejoice in the LORD;
> I will take joy in the God of my salvation.
GOD, the Lord, is my strength;
> he makes my feet like the deer's;
> he makes me tread on my high places. (3:17–19)

Putting your faith in God and trusting that justice will come is challenging when we see injustice all around. Yet our trusting in God's fairness pleases him.

7. REDEMPTION AND THE REDEEMER

The terms "salvation" and "redemption" sometimes get used interchangeably. To redeem means "to buy back." The first sign of redemption came immediately after the fall of our first parents. When Adam and Eve sewed fig leaves together and made themselves loincloths to cover their sin (Gen. 3:7), God responded by stepping in and pointing the way to redemption. He would buy us back through a sacrifice—through blood. "God made for Adam and for his wife garments of skins and clothed them" (v. 21). The skins would have presupposed shedding blood; Adam and Eve being clothed by God points to our being clothed with righteousness (Isa. 61:10; 64:6; 2 Cor. 5:21). God thus bought us back because of his great love for us.

The Father sent his Son to be the redeemer of the world. At his baptism a voice came from heaven: "This is my beloved Son, with whom I am well pleased" (Matt. 3:17). When Jesus was transfigured before his disciples, a voice from the cloud on the mountain said, "This is my beloved Son, with whom I am well pleased; listen to him" (17:5). Jesus was a man as though he were not God (John

1:14). He was God as though he were not man (v. 1). "In him all the fullness of God was pleased to dwell" (Col. 1:19).

Jesus promised to fulfill the Mosaic law (Matt. 5:17). This was, said Martyn Lloyd-Jones, the most stupendous claim Jesus ever made. He stated concerning his relationship to the Father, "I always do the things that are pleasing to him" (John 8:29). Jesus never sinned; he indeed fulfilled the law. God was at the bottom of the crucifixion, laying on Jesus "the iniquity of us all" (Isa. 53:6); thus, "it pleased the LORD to bruise him" (53:10 KJV). Jesus came to finish the work the Father gave him to do (John 4:34); consequently, just before he died on the cross he uttered these words: "It is finished" (19:30).

Faith in the blood of Jesus counts for righteousness, said the Apostle Paul (Rom. 3:25; 4:5; 5:9). On Good Friday God revealed that he was both just and merciful at the same time when the blood of Jesus propitiated his justice by turning his wrath away. Our Redeemer became our great high priest at the right hand of God; there he is seated, ever beckoning the Father to look at himself "to keep his gaze away from our sins," as Calvin put it.

Thus, God is pleased when we affirm his plan of redemption and his choice of a Redeemer.

8. The Gospel

As creation was God's idea, so also was the gospel, which means "good news." The gospel is "the power of God for *salvation*" (Rom. 1:16, emphasis mine), making us fit for heaven when we die. Jesus began his ministry by preaching the gospel of the kingdom and demonstrating the power he had to heal (Matt. 4:23). The kingdom of heaven is the rule and reign of the Holy Spirit. Jesus also laid down the foundation of the eternal gospel in the Sermon on the Mount and his parables. Finally, the gospel as articulated and upheld by Paul was based on the death and resurrection of Jesus, applying *all* of Jesus's teachings. "It pleased God through the folly of what we preach to save those who believe" (1 Cor. 1:21).

The problem Jesus's disciples had, however, was that the word "kingdom" to them meant a physical overthrowing of Rome. That is what the Israelites of Jesus's time lived for. That is how they perceived their Messiah. Convinced that Jesus was the true Messiah, they never got the physicality and visibility of the kingdom out of their heads—despite Jesus saying it is within us (Luke 17:21). After Jesus's resurrection, when his disciples asked him, "Will you at this time restore the kingdom to Israel?" (Acts 1:6)—an ill-posed question—he referred them to the Holy Spirit and introduced soul winning: "You will receive power when the Holy Spirit has come upon you, and you will be my witnesses in Jerusalem and in all Judea and Samaria, and to the end of the earth" (1:8).

Soul winning pleases God. The church must never outgrow concern for lost souls. It pleased God to save those who believe through preaching—soul winning. When you and I are engaged in talking to the lost about Jesus's death being the basis of salvation, we have God's attention. When we cool off—as the church at Ephesus had done by abandoning their first love (Rev. 2:4)—we greatly displease the Lord. If we put politics, spiritual gifts, or giving millions of dollars to God before our love for the lost, we displease him. Any person, church, group, or organization that puts preaching to the lost to one side risks losing God's favor.

9. THE HOLY SPIRIT

When Jesus introduced the Holy Spirit to his disciples, they were not pleased. Two thousand years later, some Christians are still not pleased when one speaks of the Holy Spirit. In my opinion, this is partly because those who have received the most prominence in recent years are charismatics emphasizing the Spirit over the importance of the Word. However, when the Holy Spirit came down on the day of Pentecost, the followers of Jesus knew for the first time why Jesus died and why he was raised from the dead. Jesus had said that the Holy Spirit would lead to soul winning (Acts 1:8) as his followers spread the gospel, and now they understood this. But I'm afraid too many charismatics don't know their Bibles. Nor do they appear excited about the gospel, choosing instead to fixate on the gifts of the Spirit, healing, and miracles. I am actually one of them, so I hope they might listen to what this old man has to say before he leaves this world.

When Jesus introduced the Holy Spirit, he added that there were many more things he had to say about the Spirit which his disciples were not able to bear at that time (John 16:12). The Apostle Paul provided this remaining information, showing that there are "gifts" of the Spirit (1 Cor. 12:8–10), that we must be filled with the Spirit (Eph. 5:18), and that the Spirit can be grieved (4:30) or quenched (1 Thess. 5:19).

What pleases God is faithfulness to the Word *and* the Spirit—equally. We need to know not just God's Word but also how to *experience God*. I have said at other times that there is a silent divorce in the church between the Word and the Spirit. I call it *silent* because we don't know when it happened. As divorces go, some children stay with the mother while some stay with the father. In this silent divorce in the church, there are those on the Word side and those on the Spirit side. Those on the Word side emphasize the gospel, "the faith that was once for all delivered to the saints" (Jude 3), sound theology, and knowing the

Bible backward and forward. What is wrong with that emphasis? Nothing—it is exactly right. Those who emphasize the Spirit contend that until we experience what happened in the book of Acts—where there were signs and wonders, visions, and people being miraculously healed or struck dead from lying to the Holy Spirit—the honor of God will not be restored. What is wrong with that emphasis? Nothing—it is exactly right.

My burden is this: we need both. This simultaneous combination in great measure will result in spontaneous combustion. When people go to a Word church, they go to hear. When they go to a Spirit church, they hope to see things. May God hasten the day when this becomes universal: those who go to see will hear, and those who go to hear will see.

10. THE CHURCH

The Greek word *ecclesia*—translated church—means "the called out." The word *ecclesiology* refers to the doctrine of the church, including such things as church government, offices in the church, baptism, and the Lord's Supper. But we are not talking about systematic theology here. What concerns me about the church is how the church represents God to the world.

Understanding the church is important because God's reputation—his name—is attached to the church. In the previous paragraph, I said the church is "the called out." The question arises, "Called out by whom?" Paul addresses the "called" in Romans 1:6, who are identified later on as those who had been predestined (8:30). However, Jesus also said, "Many are called, but few are chosen" (Matt. 22:14). The Greek word translated into English as "called" can refer to those who hear the preaching of the gospel outwardly. Forgive me if this gets a little confusing, but there is both an inward and outward calling. The outward call is the general preaching of the gospel to anyone listening. Those who hear the call of the gospel and believe it are the ones who hear it inwardly—when they hear the outward call, they respond: "Yes, I am a sinner and desire to repent and follow Jesus." Those called inwardly are God's elect. This is important to notice, because it indicates that in the visible church you have all those who are baptized but not regenerated (born again) and in the invisible church you have all those who are regenerated, whether baptized or not. Furthermore, we must recognize that not all who are church members are saved.

But the world does not know this. Generally speaking, most people in the world—including Muslims, Buddhists, and Hindus—don't know the difference between a Catholic and a Baptist or a liberal and an evangelical. Those in the church who recognize these things must strive to uphold the gospel, the Word, and the Spirit, and pray for an awakening that will force the world to take notice. My prayer is that the fear of God will return to the church. This is the hope of the world.

There has never been a time on this earth when the visible church of God was perfect. Revival spawned the church in Corinth—but that church was full of problems. The same was true for Galatia. Ephesus. Colosse. Fast forwarding to the sixteenth century, John Knox (1514–1572) regarded the church in Geneva during the years 1553–1558 as the "most perfect school of Christ on earth" under the influence of John Calvin. But questionable things still emerged in those days, most infamously the execution of Michael Servetus (d. 1553) because of his false teachings. During the New England Awakening (c. 1725–1750), the church saw revival but also grappled with controversial problems emerging from their lack of unity on views of baptism. I look at my old Church of the Nazarene in Ashland, Kentucky, as I grew up; it shaped me and is the reason God has used me. But it had all sorts of weird views on perfectionism, worldliness, and women's dress. I would like to believe that the next Great Awakening will help reform the church and permeate society for good—including restoring the kind of righteousness that "exalts a nation" (Prov. 14:34)—but since no Christian will be glorified until we get to heaven (Rom. 8:30; 1 John 3:2–3), there is no reason to think that perfection of the church will come to this earth before the second coming.

11. THE RESURRECTION OF THE BODY

The coming of the Son of God to the world is in two stages: the first and the second coming. He came the first time in the "fullness of time" (Gal. 4:4) some two thousand years ago, and died on a cross then rose from the dead. Jesus will come a second time and will be seen as God Almighty—the Righteous Judge. "It is appointed for man to die once, and after that comes judgment, so Christ, having been offered once to bear the sins of many, will appear a second time, not to deal with sin but to save those who are eagerly waiting for him" (Heb. 9:27–28). Simultaneous with the second coming of Jesus, then, will be the resurrection of all the dead. This means all people who ever lived—saved and lost—will be resurrected. Not merely their spirits, but also their bodies. Those who died at sea (Rev. 20:13) or who were cremated will be put together by the Creator God in a split second. Paul was not referring to salvation when he said, "As in Adam all die, so also in Christ shall all be made alive" (1 Cor. 15:22), but that all will be raised—*resurrected*—owing to the resurrection of Jesus from the dead. The resurrection of Jesus on Easter Sunday is the earnest that one day all people—saved and lost—will be raised. Those not saved will not be annihilated but will be raised, as Jesus put it, for the "resurrection of judgment" (John 5:29).

The resurrection has been the comfort of the church for two thousand years. The present life is not all there is! We have heaven to look forward to, and we will be reunited with our loved ones who have preceded us in death. It will be the moment of glorification: we will be transformed to be like Jesus (1 John 3:2). It will be the end of suffering: "He will wipe away every tear from their eyes, and death shall be no more, neither shall there be mourning, nor crying, nor pain anymore, for the former things have passed away" (Rev. 21:4). We are to comfort one another with this kind of teaching, says Paul (1 Thess. 4:18).

But the resurrection will be a day of horror for those not saved. The Apostle John gave a short preview of how the world will generally react at the second coming of Jesus: "Behold, he is coming with the clouds, and every eye will see him, even those who pierced him, and all tribes of the earth will wail on account of him. Even so. Amen" (Rev. 1:7). People who normally don't want to be seen crying or sobbing will not try to appear sophisticated or unbothered; they will know that this is the end—the day of days and the time of standing before God. Every person will be utterly alone and can take no comfort from the fact that many others will be in the same place too.

You may ask: how is God pleased when people will be eternally lost? I don't know. I do know that God gets no pleasure from the "death of the wicked" (Ezek. 33:11). I also know that there are some things that God does not want us to know. His ways are higher than our ways (Isa. 55:9). Never forget that one of the lessons of the burning bush is that there are some things God does not want us to know. We may attempt to find out why a bush is on fire but not burned up, but God says, "STOP. Don't come any closer. Take off your shoes" (see Ex. 3:5).

12. THE FINAL JUDGMENT

My dad used to say, "We will know more about heaven five minutes after we've been there than all the speculation this side of it." This is also true of the final judgment. The Bible does not tell us all we would like to know about the judgment, heaven, or hell. Thus, I try to follow the axiom, "Where the Scriptures speak, we speak; where the Scriptures are silent, we are silent."

In my old church in Ashland, Kentucky, we had three "revivals" a year—each of them lasting about ten or twelve days. Not all visiting preachers followed the same pattern, except for the final Sunday night; on that occasion the sermon subject would be— almost always—about the final judgment. It was the last attempt to get people saved who had not yet been persuaded to receive the gospel.

Hebrews 9:27 says that it is appointed for all people to die— "once, and after that comes judgment." The point of dying "once" rules out any notion of a person coming back as a different person in a future life. We will all die once, but death is not the end: we all will face the final judgment. There Jesus Christ will be the judge (2 Tim. 4:1). The final judgment will deal with two issues: (1) whether one is saved or lost and (2) those who are saved. The lost will go "into eternal punishment," the saved "into eternal life" (Matt. 25:46). Regarding the saved, some will receive a reward while some will have their works consumed by fire and receive no reward (1 Cor. 3:14–15). "We must all appear before the judgment seat of Christ, so that each one may receive what is due for what he has done in the body, whether good or evil" (2 Cor. 5:10).

Revelation 20:11 speaks of a "great white throne." This is where the "books were opened," along with "another book" called the "book of life" (v. 12). Those whose names were not written in the Book of Life were "thrown into the lake of fire" (v. 15). Would this mean annihilation of the lost? I would be content if this were true. The problem is, Revelation 20:10 says that the devil was thrown into the lake of fire to be tormented forever and ever. If hell was created for the devil and his angels (Matt. 25:41)—and the lost join them there—it would seem to me that the Bible teaches a permanent punishment. I appeal again to Genesis 18:25: "Shall not the Judge of all the earth do what is just?"

Hell is not my idea. It is God's idea. Had he asked for my advice, I would have told him, "Save everybody." I will stick to his Word—and stand by it. What is more, doing this pleases God. And that is what I care about. We must always return to Abraham's conclusion when he could not understand God's judgment: "Shall not the Judge of all the earth do what is just?" I am also reminded of the late Dr. J. I. Packer's (1926–2020) use of the word "antinomy" in his book *Evangelism and the Sovereignty of God*: two parallels that are apparently contradictory but both true. God knows who will be saved, but he urges us to try to save everybody! This teaching has been fundamental to me over the years. I have sought to save everybody I can, but at the same time I sleep like a baby at night knowing that God is in control. Do I try to figure this out? No.

The aforementioned twelve principles show generally what pleases God. He is pleased with sound teaching. He is pleased when we seek to understand his Word. He is pleased when we worship him as he is revealed to us in Scripture.

The purpose of this book is to motivate you to want to please God. As you read, if you feel that you have failed in this endeavor, let me remind you of something C. S. Lewis said: "You can't go back and change the beginning, but you can start where you are and change the ending."

As surely as you are alive, you can begin anew. God is on your side.

CHAPTER 3

WHAT DISPLEASES GOD?

❧

With most of them God was not pleased, for they were over-thrown in the wilderness.

—1 CORINTHIANS 10:5

It is sad to find so many professing Christians who appear to regard the wrath of God as something for which to apologize.

—A. W. PINK (1886–1952)

I have heard it said: "I believe in heaven, but I don't believe in hell." If there is no hell, there is no heaven. Whatever makes us think we can rightly believe in heaven? Is heaven our fanciful wish? Is it, as the German philosopher Ludwig Feuerbach (1804–1872) argued, man's projection upon the backdrop of the universe?

No sane human being would come up with the notion of hell as it is depicted in Holy Scripture. This is God's idea. It is not our projection. Not our fancy. Not our wish.

How can a loving, just God conceive of the idea of eternal punishment in hell? My only reply is this: His ways are higher than our ways and his thoughts higher than our thoughts (Isa. 55:9). I trust him. I trust his judgment. I trust his faithfulness. I trust his worth. His honor. His Word. This is what pleases God. Not to believe his Word—however difficult it is to understand—displeases him.

You will say: how can a just God expect reasonable human beings to accept what seems—at least on the surface—to be preposterous, unkind, and unfair?

I will answer: Once the Spirit of God grips our hearts through regeneration—that is, being born again—we begin to think like God thinks. Thinking God's thoughts is a process. God is patient with us. He knows how we think and how we feel.

The two things I wish to convey in this chapter are: (1) how unbelief displeases God and (2) how rejecting the Scriptures we don't like displeases God. The New Testament view of Scripture is that "all" Scripture is inspired by the Holy Spirit (2 Tim. 3:16). God is not like a restaurant which we might patronize and pick and choose what we want to eat. He wants us to accept Holy Scripture as being from him—all of it. And he wants us to embrace Scripture in its entirety. Embracing the entire Bible as the true Word of God brings him pleasure, honor, and glory.

How do we know that unbelief displeases God? In Hebrews 11:6 the word about Enoch pleasing God is followed by these words: "without faith it is impossible to please him, for whoever would draw near to God must believe that he exists." (The King James Version puts it this way: "he is.") This verse teaches at least three things. First, without faith it is impossible to please God. This means that we may do amazing things, but if these things are not produced by faith they get nowhere with God. We are saved by faith plus nothing. But, surely, the Hebrew Christians already had faith—otherwise, why would the writer be addressing them? True. Then why does he add that we must believe that God "exists" or "is"? There is thus a second thing Hebrews 11:6 teaches us. These Hebrew Christians were in the middle of a great time of trial and testing. They were discouraged. Their numbers were dwindling. Vindication that they had got things right had been withheld from them. This is why the writer seeks to encourage them over and over again in his letter. But why does he bother to say that discouraged people need to believe that God exists? The answer is this: there is not a saint on this planet who does not experience the satanic suggestion in a time of deep trial, "See there—there is no God, or he would not have let these things happen." If there were a living God who cares and is all-powerful, there would be no suffering, no evil, no COVID-19, and no horrible accidents. This is when the believer must stand up and say, "I believe God. I believe that he is. That he exists. That he is in control. And that he has a purpose in what he has allowed." *That is what pleases God!*

The third thing Hebrews 11:6 teaches is that God *rewards* those who seek him. Some versions say, "Diligently seek him" (KJV, NKJV). Having faith, believing God exists, and believing that God rewards those who pursue him keeps us from displeasing him. I do not want to displease the Lord. I want to find out what pleases him. That means seeking him. We seek when we need to look beyond the surface. Seeking takes time and effort. It means you don't give up.

I have come across a good number of Christians who believe it is not becoming to want a reward. One close friend thinks we should be "above" wanting a reward from God—that we should serve God without any thought of reward! What should we say to people who believe something like this?

First, Hebrews 11:6 does promise a reward for seeking God—whether some like it or not! Second, Hebrews 11:26 states that a reward is what encouraged Moses to keep pressing on after leaving the palace of the king. Not only that; even Jesus was partly motivated to endure the cross because of the "joy that was set before him" (12:2)!

God made us in such a way that we all are naturally motivated by some kind of reward. The call of Abraham was accompanied by the promise that God would make Abraham's name great and whoever cursed him would be cursed (Gen. 12:2–3). I would call that a pretty strong motivation! The truth is, God always does this. Even when under the period of the Mosaic law, which emphasized obedience, God stooped to motivate tithers with a blessing so great that they could not contain it (Mal. 3:10–12). Jesus consistently linked his commands to promises for those who obeyed them. If we don't judge, we won't be judged; if we forgive, we will be forgiven. Keeping the commands of the Sermon on the Mount will result in incalculable blessing (Luke 6:37–38) and assurance that we will be able to stand and survive when the severe storm comes (Matt. 7:24–25).

TWELVE PRINCIPLES THAT DISPLEASE GOD

Sometimes we learn by studying a subject's opposite. To know more fully about what pleases God, we now look at twelve principles that displease God. There are more things that displease

God than the following list shows. Moreover, some sins displease him more than other sins while not all sins are equally as bad in his sight or ours. This list is not hierarchical, so don't read too much into the order.

1. BELIEVERS WHO COMMIT ADULTERY

I have heard people say, "If someone commits adultery, they are not believers." Really? Was King David a believer? Of course he was. The Bible says twice that David was a man after God's own heart (1 Sam. 13:14; Acts 13:22). David's sin is arguably the most horrible described in the entire Bible—both adultery and murder. But when Nathan confronted him, David was not defensive but instantly repented—and wrote Psalm 51. Paul even quoted David's words in Psalm 32:2—"Blessed is the man against whom the LORD counts no iniquity"—in Romans 4:8. And yet "the thing that David had done displeased the LORD" (2 Sam. 11:27). Never doubt this: not only is sanctification God's unmistakable will (1 Thess. 4:3) but "the Lord is an avenger in all these things" (v. 6).

Dear reader, I lovingly warn you, if you commit adultery, "be sure your sin will find you out" (Num. 32:23). It is only a matter of time before you will be sorry. Very, very sorry. And if you are in an affair right now, I say: break it off—now. If you don't, you will one day give anything for a chance to turn the clock back to this moment when God is speaking to you through these very lines.

By the way, David paid dearly for his sin. Sexual sin does not necessarily displease God more than other transgressions listed in this section. I list it first because this is almost certainly what brings greater dishonor and shame upon the church than the other sins. I also list it first because so many Christian leaders have been and are falling into this sin in ever-increasing numbers.

Every week, it seems some preacher is found out. I once heard Billy Graham say, "It seems that the devil gets seventy-five percent of God's best servants through sexual temptation." Having said these things, I encourage those who read these lines and who have sinned in this way to take heart from the words of Bernard of Clairvaux (1090–1153):

> O hope of every contrite heart, O Joy of all
>   the meek,
> To those who fall, how kind Thou art, How good to
>   those who seek.

Hear too the words of the same King David after he was found out by Nathan the prophet:

> The sacrifices of God are a broken spirit;
>   a broken and contrite heart, O God, you will
>   not despise. (Ps. 51:17)

2. RACISM

It is impossible to know which evil from my list of sins here is the worst in God's sight. I did not list racism first because I do not want this book to be seen as political. But it is my personal opinion that the way black people on both sides of the Atlantic have been treated has angered God as much as any other wickedness in the entire world. (As a theologian I have learned from Holy Scripture that *the angrier God is, the longer he takes to show it.*) I believe that the judgment God is inflicting on America is largely due to racism. Of course, God is angry with us because we have turned our back on him as a nation. Granted. But a strain running through the Bible that many of us don't want to be convinced of is this: God is for the underdog. This includes rich, poor, black, and white. I know how I myself felt for years, and am ashamed to say this. But it is how I know how many Americans feel. Not only have we treated black people with either a benign neglect or outright contempt, but it does not bother many of us. We white people have no idea what black people have gone through and continue to go through. Most of us have no idea how black people feel— nor do we want to know. An illustration of this is the testimony of a popular American black comedian who spent two weeks in Ghana. He said that for the first time in his life he felt like a white person. He was never conscious of the color of his skin even once during those two weeks. The late Joel Edwards, born in Jamaica, who was president of the Evangelical Alliance in England—and greatly loved—told me that he never once went outside his house in London without being conscious that he was black. But God knows how black people feel. Jesus knows. Frankly, I don't know what it will take—if anything—that will change the way many white people think—and I include many white Christians. I do know that *black people matter to Jesus*. Of course white people matter to him. Also Japanese. Koreans. Indians. Puerto Ricans. But no group in my lifetime has suffered like African Americans. God is displeased at this.

3. Esteeming the Praise of People More Than the Approval of God

Have you ever wondered how Israel could reject their own Messiah two thousand years ago? Read on. But, first, in 1956 the

49

words of Jesus in John 5:44 gripped me for some reason: "How can ye believe, which receive honour one of another, and seek not the honour that cometh from God only?" (KJV). Most translations say "the only God," but it comes to the same thing. John 5:44 has become my "life verse," although I would never say I have always been governed by it. It is a very high standard. That said, John 5:44 has been my chief motivation in life. It has also kept me from making stupid mistakes. It has encouraged me when I have had to make unpopular but hard decisions. John 5:44—addressed to Jews generally and Pharisees particularly—shows the main reason that the Jews missed their Messiah two thousand years ago. Jesus accused them of preferring the honor of people over the glory and honor of God and diagnosed their problem: they were consequently *unable* to believe. Their fear of man ended up blinding them. They missed their Messiah. They forgot that God is a jealous God. They did not think that God noticed when they lived mainly for the approval of others. In contrast, Jesus revealed how his Father felt about them. It was the moment of moments when the opinion of heaven about Israel was brought out. The John 5:44 principle exists today in showing that many miss what God would do in their lives because they worry more about what people think than what God thinks.

Let me say this to you when it comes to John 5:44 (or any Scripture, for that matter): You will stand *alone* at the judgment seat of Christ. Those who may have influenced you won't be around. It will be you by yourself standing before Jesus Christ. Thus, I pray that the John 5:44 principle will grip you and make a profound difference in your life. As we will see in Part III of this book, the approval of God may be demonstrated in two ways: here on earth and at the final judgment.

4. BEING ASHAMED OF THE GOSPEL

We are often ashamed of the stigma. It amounts to this: embracing embarrassment. But God is displeased when we run from embarrassment rather than witness for his Son. Both Jesus and Paul cautioned people to not be ashamed of the truth. Jesus said, "Whoever is ashamed of me *and of my words* in this adulterous and sinful generation, of him will the Son of Man also be ashamed when he comes in the glory of his Father with the holy angels" (Mark 8:38, emphasis mine). Paul added, "I am not ashamed of the gospel, for it is the power of God for salvation to everyone who believes, to the Jew first and also to the Greek" (Rom. 1:16). Paul included himself when he said to Timothy, "Do not be ashamed of the testimony about our Lord, nor of me his prisoner" (2 Tim. 1:8).

Why do you suppose the concern about being "ashamed" would come up often? Answer: Because of fear and pride. We are afraid of the cost when certain people find out we are Christians. We are afraid of the cost—to our pride and our financial security—when certain people find out what it is we believe! The *words* of Jesus cover sensitive topics such as acknowledging, or confessing, him before people (Matt. 10:32); being persecuted for his sake (5:11); and people going into "outer darkness" where there will be "weeping and gnashing of teeth" (8:12).

Dear reader, never apologize to anyone for the biblical teaching of the wrath of God; Jesus had more words to say about this than anyone else in the Bible. He calls us to deny ourselves, take up our cross, and follow him, even to the point of losing our lives (Mark 8:34–35). God is displeased when we are ashamed of his Son. He is disappointed when we don't tell our friends or neighbors about Jesus—why he came, why he died, and what the consequences of not believing and confessing him openly are. So, we need to confidently declare that Jesus is the only way to God. One of the best reasons for giving an altar call or calling for public confession after preaching is that the new believer can be launched into the Christian faith by coming out of hiding and admitting publicly his belief in Jesus. Josif Ton told me that in Romania—in the days of Communism—the offense of even raising your hand to confess Christ was greater than a person being baptized.

5. ABORTIONS

God hates abortions. He is displeased with abortion being legal so that people can choose not to keep their children. Two things especially sicken me: men and women using these abortion laws to have sex without taking on the responsibility of children and the reprehensible dilemmas other women face when they are pressured to have abortions (whether because of difficult economic circumstances or coercion from others). Lust—sex apart from marriage—primarily lies behind the evil of abortion. If people did not have the desire for sex without taking on the responsibility of children, I doubt *anyone* would deny that life truly begins at conception. I cannot imagine anything more obvious! But sexual appetite has controlled public thinking. To say arbitrarily that life begins after three months of pregnancy, six months of pregnancy, or when birth takes place shows what one *chooses* to believe, not what the Bible clearly says. When the baby who would later become John the Baptist leaped in Elizabeth's womb when she greeted the Virgin Mary (Luke 1:41), this showed that the Son of God as an embryo in Mary's womb was a human being. When David affirmed to God, "Your eyes saw my unformed substance; in your book were written, every one of them, the days that were formed for me, when as yet there was none of them" (Ps. 139:16), he demonstrated that his unformed substance was *living*.

I believe that God's judgment lies on America partly because of legalized abortions. Those who uphold "pro-choice" rather than "pro-life" say that they have a *right* to choose. Wrong. "You are not your own," said Paul, "you were bought with a price," namely, the blood of Christ (1 Cor. 6:19–20). If you say that verse applies only to Christians, I reply: Jesus tasted death for every person (Heb. 2:9); he died for all (2 Cor. 5:15). I don't mean to be unfair, but it seems to me that senators, congresspeople, ministers, and politicians have a lot to answer for. They should repent for the laws upholding abortion that have been passed. We should all be ashamed that public opinion has shifted as it has.

My heart goes out to women who have had abortions and have since suffered incalculable remorse. Here are my words to *anyone* reading these lines who feels deep, deep guilt for *any* past sin: God is a merciful God. He is a forgiving God. He not only totally forgives you, but wants you to forgive yourself—totally. I have written a book, *Totally Forgiving Ourselves*, endorsed by the same J. I. Packer I mentioned earlier. Never forget good old 1 John 1:9: when we sin, "[God] is faithful and just to forgive us our sins and to cleanse us from all unrighteousness."

6. SAME-SEX MARRIAGE

As recently as ten years ago, the American public generally was against same-sex marriage. But nowadays same-sex marriage has been accepted generally—nearly everywhere in the USA. As with abortion, homosexual practice is clearly condemned in Holy Scripture. There are two views I should mention: (1) "The Bible is of course against homosexual marriage, but I don't believe the

Bible in the first place"; and (2) "Jesus would accept homosexual practice." In 1988 I wrote a book, *Is God for the Homosexual?* Answer: Yes. It was endorsed by the bishop of London, Graham Leonard. The homosexual community in London felt that the book showed genuine sympathy and understanding for gay people without condemning them. But they ultimately rejected the book because I did condemn homosexual practice and said that such people should abstain, just as any heterosexual person must abstain from sex before marriage. The Mosaic law condemned homosexual practice (Lev. 18:22), and the punishment for such a sin was the same as adultery—death (Deut. 22:22–24). We need to soberly accept what God says on this matter.

Those who think that Jesus would accept homosexual practice need to ask, would he accept adultery too? After all, Jesus said to the woman found in adultery, though he did not condemn her, "From now on sin no more" (John 8:11). Jesus's compassion does not mean that he approves of behavior God has forbidden. Same-sex marriage is not only legalizing homosexual practice but giving it a sanctity and dignity that would have been unthinkable by most people only a few years ago.

These things said, I do believe Christians should show sympathy and understanding toward the person struggling with a homosexual proclivity; he or she cannot help it. Jesus sympathizes with every weakness (Heb. 4:15). So should we.

7. THEOLOGICAL LIBERALISM

Theological liberalism in pulpits is not new. Harry Emerson Fosdick (1878–1969), pastor of Riverside Church in New York City, was famous for attacking fundamentalists and denying the virgin birth of Jesus: "Of course I do not believe in the virgin birth and I don't know of any intelligent minister who does." Nels F. S. Ferré (1908–71), a universalist and professor at Vanderbilt University, posed the possibility that Jesus could have been the bastard son of a German soldier in the Roman army and also said, "If God would send anyone to hell, I would want to be that person."

Universities like Harvard and Yale were founded by Puritans. The motto of Harvard is *Veritas*—"truth," and the motto of Yale is *Lux et veritas*—"Light and truth." These universities are now famous for their theological liberalism. But even many evangelical colleges and seminaries have become liberal partly because they wanted to impress the Harvards and Yales of this world—to show them that they are not stupid. They opted for biblical criticism, claiming that the Bible should be studied like one would study Shakespeare. I would be surprised if there is a single professor in the so-called Ivy League universities who believes in the deity of Jesus, the virgin birth, salvation only by the blood of Christ, the bodily resurrection of Jesus, and the need to be born again.

As a consequence of this, churches across America are filled with pastors who do not believe people need to be saved. A phenomenon called "open theism"—which could be called atheism in disguise—has also influenced many evangelicals and charismatics. Many people don't know this term. But it is held by ministers who believe God has no will or ability to do things apart from human actions. According to open theism, God's knowledge of the future is totally dependent on our help in figuring out what happens next. These views are alien to the God of the Bible. I often think that God's judgment on America began with the rise of liberal ministers who disdain the fact that America was founded with a widespread sense of the fear of God and respect for the Bible as the word of God.

8. THE SIN UNTO DEATH

The sin unto death is the Apostle John's depiction of Christians dying before their time, as it were (1 John 5:16). The Apostle Paul also needed to explain to the Corinthian Christians why some of them were weak, sickly, and even dead. In that case, it was because they had abused the Lord's Supper by treating their poor brothers and sisters with astonishing disrespect (1 Cor. 11:17–22). God is for the underdog. The well-to-do believers should have waited for the poor people who arrived late for the Lord's Supper, but they instead treated them as outsiders, excluding them from the holy meal. They thought no one noticed—but God saw this. They then began wondering why some of them were dying. Having shown these believers their huge mistake, Paul said: "That is why many of you are weak and ill, and some have died" (v. 30). Paul proved that these were truly Christians who needed to be harshly chastened in saying, "If we judged ourselves truly, we would not be judged. But when we are judged by the Lord, we are disciplined so that we may not be condemned along with the world" (vv. 31–32).

Another example of the sin unto death is God's striking down of Ananias and Sapphira. They were not only greedy but also wanted to be seen as "very in" with the church, which is why they lied to Peter regarding the sale of their property (Acts 5:1–11). I take the view that if we were in a revival situation today, things that happened in the earliest days of the church such as this visible example of God's discipline would return. In the meantime, I'm sure many believers have abused the Lord's Supper since then— plus repeating the sin of Ananias and Sapphira—with no apparent consequence. There are, however, sins that do not lead to death (1 John 5:16ff). It is not clear to me what other sins can lead to death. In the end, we can thank God once more for 1 John 1:9: "If we confess our sins, he is faithful and just to forgive us our sins and to cleanse us from all unrighteousness." As long as God grants us repentance—being changed from glory to glory (2 Cor. 3:18)—we may be sure we have not committed the sin that leads to death.

9. INGRATITUDE, COMPLAINING, AND A FEELING OF ENTITLEMENT

A feeling of entitlement is a virus that has spread everywhere. We live in the "What's in it for me?" generation—the "me decade," as one writer put it. The origin of the feeling of entitlement is in ingratitude, and this is not new to the twenty-first century. God loves gratitude and he hates ingratitude—but gratitude must be taught. For example, the reason for the Lord's Supper is to remind us that God sent Jesus to die on the cross for us; it teaches us to be thankful (1 Cor. 11:24).

We all tend to forget how good God has been to us, and our ingratitude gets his attention. Unthankfulness was listed in the group of horrible sins described in Romans 1 (see vv. 18–32). Grumbling was listed alongside the heinous sins that character-ized the people of ancient Israel who failed to enter the promised land (1 Cor. 10:10). When Jesus healed ten lepers, only one came back to give thanks. Jesus's only response was this: "Were not ten cleansed? Where are the nine?" (Luke 17:17). The Apostle Paul said that prayer should be carried out "with thanksgiving" (Phil. 4:6). He also warned that people would be ungrateful in the last days (2 Tim. 3:2).

I fear that so much "health and wealth" preaching encourages people to try to force God to give us what he owes us! No worse atti-tude toward God is imaginable. We should take a lesson from the leper who came to Jesus in Mark 1. The leper knew his place; he did not approach Jesus with the expectation, "You have to heal me." No. Instead, he said to Jesus: "If you will"—as if to say, "you don't have to"—"you can make me clean." Jesus replied, "I will" (vv. 40–41). In line with this, the first thing we should ask for when we pray is "mercy" (Heb. 4:16), remembering that God said to Moses, "[I] will show mercy on whom I will show mercy" (Ex. 33:19).

The Mayo Clinic came out with a statement not long ago: "Thankful people live longer." As children of God, we should be the most thankful people of all.

10. UNFORGIVENESS

We all have a story to tell. There is no one on this planet who has not at some stage been mistreated, betrayed, or lied about. The most natural feeling in the world is a sense of hurt and anger toward those who have done us harm. It seems right, after all. However, as Jesus equated lusting after a woman to committing adultery in the heart, so too did he accuse us of murder when we are angry and don't forgive (Matt. 5:21–26). Why is unforgiveness so terrible? First, it grieves the Holy Spirit. As soon as Paul cautioned us not to grieve the Holy Spirit of God, he added "bitterness" as the first thing that so often grieves the Spirit. He went on to equate it with anger and unforgiveness (Eph. 4:30–32). Second, holding a grudge gives place to the devil. Satan, the archenemy of Jesus Christ—and your archenemy as well—is looking for an entry point into our hearts and lives each day and night. When we refuse to forgive and maintain a spirit of unforgiveness, we unwittingly invite the devil to move in. Paul said of Satan, "We are not ignorant of his devices" (2 Cor. 2:11 KJV; "designs," ESV). Additionally, the first sin committed after Adam and Eve fell was when an angry Cain killed his brother Abel (Gen. 4:8). What happens, then, when we don't forgive or hold a grudge? The Spirit is grieved and withdraws the sense of his presence—the anointing. I have learned that God won't bend the rules for anyone! As I said before, many feel justified in holding a grudge. The backslider is "filled with his own ways" (Prov. 14:14 KJV).

Speaking personally, I justified feeling resentful about my hurt for years. God mercifully and graciously woke me up, and my life was changed forever. Perhaps this needs to happen to you, too? I urge you: forgive those who hurt you; let them off the hook and start praying for them—and mean it. I don't say this will be easy. But forgiveness is the best advice I have ever received. Perhaps that is what will emerge from reading this book. As Josif Ton said to me, "Totally forgive them; release them, or you will remain in chains."

11. SELF-RIGHTEOUSNESS AND SELF-PITY

These twin sins are almost certainly the hardest to see in ourselves. Whereas all sin is blinding—and only the Holy Spirit can make anyone see his or her sin—self-righteousness is impossible to see in oneself. I can see it in you, but I cannot see it in me! One reason God hates self-righteousness so much is because it is the chief enemy of the gospel. It is the reason why people do not see their need for a Savior. This is why the first work of the Holy Spirit, according to Jesus, is to "convict the world" of sin (John 16:8). The Apostle John has self-righteousness partly in mind when he plainly says to all believers, "If we say we have no sin, we deceive ourselves, and the truth is not in us" (1 John 1:8). Seeing the glory of God made Isaiah see his self-righteousness (Isa. 6:1–5). Likewise, we are loath to admit it when self-pity is the true explanation. As the backslider is "filled with the fruit of his ways" (Prov. 14:14), so do we tend to justify self-pity—which is really self-righteousness. When King David feigned mourning for his son Absalom (2 Sam. 19:1–4), his close friend, Joab, was the one who saw the real problem that had paralyzed David—self-pity. The proof that self-pity was the main issue and David's grief was phony is that when Joab made him see he was about to lose his kingship yet again, David snapped out of his paralysis in seconds (vv. 5–8). When we ponder David's adultery and murder, one wonders why David could not see his unthinkable sin immediately. About two years passed before Nathan confronted David. All that time David felt no sense of sin; his self-righteousness gave him a feeling of ease.

Self-righteousness is thus a most dangerous sin, and one which Satan will keep us from recognizing. Indeed, the "god of this world" blinds unbelievers to "the light of the knowledge of the glory of God in the face of Jesus Christ" (2 Cor. 4:4–6). A further illustration of this aspect of human depravity is that when self-righteousness is the sin that causes a believer to be overtaken (Gal. 6:1), he or she becomes the hardest person on the planet to reach. Thus, our self-righteous blindness is something which you and I can never see in ourselves unless God uses someone—whether a Nathan or Joab—to reveal it to us.

12. UNBELIEF

Another word for unbelief is atheism. God's number one task in reaching humankind is to transcend natural atheism—unbelief. Whereas the conscience of a person—also called natural revelation—is what leaves him or her without excuse, only the preaching of the gospel by the power of the Holy Spirit can save that person. "For since, in the wisdom of God, the world did not know God through wisdom, it pleased God through the folly of what we preach to save those who believe" (1 Cor. 1:21). The teaching of apologetics, which refers not to apologizing for God but to the defense of the gospel, does not save people. It may leave them without excuse, but no one comes to the Father unless drawn by the Spirit (John 6:44). The classic Reformed teaching of total depravity, better stated as *total inability*, means that all people are born spiritually "dead" (Eph. 2:1). Only the Holy Spirit "quickens": makes alive. And yet even after a person is genuinely saved, he or she can be tempted to doubt.

The ancient Israelites came short of their inheritance due to "unbelief" (Heb. 3:19). Therefore, the writer addressing Christian Hebrews says that "without faith it is impossible to please [God]," then adds: "Whoever would draw near to God must believe that he exists" (11:6). Strange comment? No. There is not a saint on earth who does not at some point have the devil say to them, "See there—there is no God, or this would not have happened." What are you and I to do then? I answer: *Stand your ground*. A trial coming out of the blue is to be expected. Do not listen to Satan! Resist him. God hates unbelief.

The essence of nearly every trial will at some stage contain the thought *there must not be a God*. This is your opportunity—handed to you on a silver platter—to say, "I believe God! The Lord rebuke you, Satan. I believe God, and I know he is a rewarder of those who diligently seek him." Stay there, reader. Hold your ground. And guess what happens next? God shows up—never too late, never too early, but always just on time.

So far in this book, I have tried to explain what pleases God and what displeases him. Yet I am aware of many unanswered questions. That is why this book is not finished! I turn now to Part II: why we should please God.

PART II

WHY SHOULD WE
PLEASE GOD?

CHAPTER 4

GOD'S DISCIPLINE

—❦—

*Why have you despised the word of the LORD, to do what
is evil in his sight? You have struck down Uriah the Hittite
with the sword and have taken his wife to be your wife and
have killed him with the sword of the Ammonites. Now therefore the sword shall never depart from your house, because
you have despised me and have taken the wife of Uriah the
Hittite to be your wife. Thus says the LORD, "Behold, I will
raise up evil against you out of your own house. And I will
take your wives before your eyes and give them to your neighbor, and he shall lie with your wives in the sight of this sun.
For you did it secretly, but I will do this thing before all Israel
and before the sun." David said to Nathan, "I have sinned
against the LORD." And Nathan said to David, "The LORD
also has put away your sin; you shall not die. Nevertheless,
because by this deed you have utterly scorned the LORD, the
child who is born to you shall die."*

—2 SAMUEL 12:9–14

*He remembers our frame and knows that we are dust. He
may sometimes chasten us, it is true, but even this He does
with a smile, the proud, tender smile of a Father who is
bursting with pleasure over an imperfect but promising son
who is coming every day to look more and more like the One
whose child he is.*

—A. W. TOZER (1897–1963)

In April 1956 I prayed a strange prayer. I had just heard a moving
sermon on Philippians 2:5–11 by Dr. Hugh C. Benner, general
superintendent in the Church of the Nazarene, at the First Church
of the Nazarene in Nashville. He spoke of how Jesus became the
lowest possible shame for the glory of God. I was so impacted
by his message that I fell to my knees and literally prayed: "God,
make me the lowest possible shame for your glory." As I have
reread this sentence, I was debating whether to leave it in or take it
out. I realize it seems odd. I am not saying I would pray this same
prayer again. But, rightly or wrongly, it is what I prayed. Whether
this was a good prayer or an unwise prayer is debatable. Was I
overly conscientious? Is it possible to be too anxious to please the
Lord? You tell me. But I prayed it. I meant it. And yet the possibility
of it being answered was remote. I was on top of the world. I was
a popular student at Trevecca Nazarene College. I was assistant to
Dr. W. M. Greathouse, the dean of religion at Trevecca. I was pastor of the Church of the Nazarene in Palmer, Tennessee. I had seen
visions indicating I would have a ministry that would go around
the world. I was driving a new Chevrolet that my grandmother
had purchased for me. How could I become a shame? This seemed
very unlikely.

But this prayer was answered. Within four months, my grand-mother took the car back. A member of my family called me a shame and disgrace. My father said I would have to pay rent to live at home. "You have broken with God," he told me. Virtually all my Nazarene friends distanced themselves from me. What had I done to bring this about? Two things: (1) a theological change that resulted from the experience of the Holy Spirit I mentioned in chapter 1, and (2) I felt led to stand by Billy Ball, the assistant pastor of my home church in Ashland, Kentucky, who had been fired by the church board because he was seen as siding with three laypeople in the church over the pastor; the pastor had not wanted revival in that church.

I was forced to get a secular job because I had embraced this new-to-me theology of the Holy Spirit. I began driving a truck to deliver and pick up clothes that needed to be dry cleaned at Cremens Quality Cleaners in Ashland. I eventually became a salesman for baby equipment—called Stroll-O-Chair. I was such a successful salesman that I won a contest rewarding me with a ticket to see *My Fair Lady* in the Dominion Theatre on Broadway (now the location for Times Square Church) in New York. I was still selling Stroll-O-Chairs when I married Louise. Next, we moved to Florida where I sold life insurance. Eventually I became a door-to-door vacuum cleaner salesman. Unfortunately, I let success go to my head and became foolish. I bought a Cessna air-plane, a new Edsel automobile when that model first came out, nice clothes, and a hi-fi set. If only I had never gone into debt for all these! Surely I was not pleasing God in those days. Why did he allow it? At what point did I make the wrong turn?

I have learned this from Romans 8:28: "For those who love God all things work together for good." However, this does not mean what we did was right at that time. For me, the good that I learned was how to handle money. I could add many other things that gave me invaluable experience, such as how to be a good businessman and how to deal with all kinds of people— rich and poor. I paid for my own radio program called *Redeemer's Witness* and had a small magazine by the same name that went to hundreds of people. I received invitations to preach in at least ten different denominations. Yes, Romans 8:28 is true, but I still paid severely for foolish mistakes, especially by going into debt.

I am truly afraid to say whether I was right or wrong in praying to be abjectly shamed. One of my greatest fears that remains—and among my greatest mistakes in life—has been to run ahead of God while assuming I was following him, which hindsight later proved false. I appeal to 1 Corinthians 4:5: "Do not pronounce judgment before the time, before the Lord comes, who will bring to light the things now hidden in darkness and will disclose the purposes of the heart. Then each one will receive his commendation from God." I know for sure that I have certainly been wrong when I thought I was right many times since praying that prayer. This is an easy thing to do.

We may also learn this from Joseph and Mary. They frequently traveled with Jesus during his childhood. On one occasion when they were returning to Galilee from Jerusalem, Jesus "stayed behind in Jerusalem," but his parents "did not know it." Joseph and Mary went a day's journey "supposing him to be in the group." Then they searched for him among their relatives and acquaintances. After failing to find him, they went back to Jerusalem to look for him there (Luke 2:41–45).

When we get used to a sense of God's presence, we may begin

to assume he is with us in our decisions since we have felt unmistakably that we were led by him up to now. We may then carry on without any worry as to whether we are being led by him. Dangerously, this can lead to feelings of entitlement. That is what happened with Jesus's parents in Luke 2. Even Mary rebuked Jesus after finding him in the temple: "Son, why have you treated us so?" (v. 48). She blamed him!

This sort of thing can happen to you and me when we forget to acknowledge God carefully and consistently in "*all* your ways" (Prov. 3:6, emphasis mine). Then we wake up—at last—realizing we were wrong to think we had some sort of a claim—or right—on God in our relationship with him.

Joshua saw an austere figure with a drawn sword in Jericho after Israel crossed the Jordan River. He asked this person: "Are you for us, or for our adversaries?" (Josh. 5:13). Joshua was about to learn something new from God and about God. Nobody had been closer to God than Joshua. He had stood with God against the majority of the Israelites some forty years earlier when they were attempting to enter the Promised Land (Num. 13:30–33). He had been chosen to succeed Moses (Deut. 31:7ff). But Joshua still had more—much more—to learn about the true God. The "commander of the army of the LORD," as the mysterious figure turned out to be, replied to Joshua's question: "No" (Josh. 5:14; "Neither" NIV). He was on the side of neither! But why? This seemed unfair. Surely the commander of the Lord's army was on Israel's side! How does one explain this?

I once asked one of my earliest mentors, Dr. N. B. Magruder (1914–2005), "Is not the highest devotion to God proved by one being a martyr for the Lord?" He smiled, then wrote a note that

I have carried with me for years: "My willingness to forsake any claim upon God is the only evidence that I have seen the Divine glory." This was and remains the profoundest comment I have ever come across in my entire life. Agree or disagree, his point was exactly the same as the Lord's word to Joshua. Joshua felt he had a claim upon God, as if God owed him something. But he was so wrong. Joshua had to learn that God owes no one anything, no matter how close we may think we are to God. However, he passed the test. Instead of arguing with God—or demanding something from him—Joshua took off his sandals and worshipped. He knew he was on holy ground (5:15).

Joshua's acceptance of a God of glory pleased the Lord. God is pleased when we affirm him as he is. He is also pleased when our greatest urge is to please him more than anyone or anything—when we seek his praise and approval and are not influenced by what people say (John 5:44).

Joshua came to see this aspect of the God of glory through what I call *internal* chastening, or disciplining. My own coming to see God in this way has taken much longer than it apparently took for Joshua. God has graciously brought me through long periods of waiting in order to get my attention and to absorb what he is like. To this day, I am still learning.

THE ULTIMATE SATISFACTION

Why please God? Because this gives to you and me an unsurpassable level of satisfaction. It feels so good when we live for pleasing God. Not to be admired by friends—or enemies—or mentors. Not for money—or for a promotion—or prestigious connections—or more open doors. Not for approval of people we don't know. But for God's approval alone. This is actualizing the point Jesus was making in John 5:44: "How can you believe, when you receive glory from one another and do not seek the glory that comes from the only God?" That is exactly what Enoch had going for him (Heb. 11:5).

Back to my story. It was now a hot August afternoon in 1956. I lay on my grandmother's bed in distress. I felt deserted not only by my family but by God. My grief was not so much over "Ma," as I called my grandmother, taking the car back (which she had a right to do). Or my father asking me to pay rent to stay at home (which he had a right to do). But it was because I sincerely had believed I would have their happy approval once they heard about my visions that led to my change of theology. I had gotten that wrong.

I remembered my prayer from that April a few months earlier as I lay on the bed that afternoon and kept hearing the words "Hebrews 12:6." I had no idea what they meant. I opened the little New Testament that I always carried with me: "Whom the Lord loveth he chasteneth, and scourgeth every son whom he receiveth" (KJV). As far as I know, this verse had never gotten my attention before. This was my introduction to the doctrine of chastening, or disciplining.

Was I being *chastened*? So it would seem. But why? What had I done? I was aware of my unworthiness and had incorporated 1 John 1:8 ("If we say we have no sin, we deceive ourselves") into my understanding of human nature. But had I committed any particular sin? If so, when or where and what was it? I had kept myself pure sexually. I had not spent money unwisely. Had Hebrews 12:6 been given to me supernaturally a year later—in 1957—when I was deep in debt, it would have made more sense to me. But Hebrews 12:6 came when I owed no one a penny.

This was, as I said, my introduction to the doctrine of chastening. I concluded eventually that chastening was essentially *preparation*. Chastening does not necessarily happen because we have done wrong, but because God is preparing us for something. Over the succeeding years I would learn a lot more, and that is what I shall share in the remainder of this chapter.

Although I had experienced chastening despite not committing any obvious sin, as I began to explore what the Bible teaches I saw that chastening is more likely to come *after* one has erred. In any case, then, here is another reason for pleasing God: because displeasing him can bring about chastening—which can be very, very painful. You may say: pleasing God to avoid being chastened by him is not a very noble motive. Granted. But the Word of God tells us that he himself wants us to be motivated in this manner. The fear of chastening is a good reason to avoid displeasing God.

The Greek word in Hebrews 12:6 meaning "discipline"—or "chasten"—is *paidenei*. It originally referred to the education of children, emphasizing *enforced learning*. A child needs disciplining from a very early age. This type of discipline teaches one a lesson. Thus, when God chastens—or chastises—us, this is akin to his saying: "I am going to teach you a lesson." But Hebrews 12:6 adds another Greek word—*mastegoi*—which means "to scourge; to whip with thongs." Therefore, God's disciplining is not pleasant! It hurts—and it can hurt a lot.

One must not forget that our heavenly Father is a jealous God.

He owns us. We are bought with a price—the blood of his Son. He is determined that we stay on the straight and narrow way!

Returning to my question, why then would God chasten me, beginning in the summer of 1956, when I was seemingly innocent? My best answer is this: (1) he sees the end from the beginning—he knows what we are capable of and what we are prone to do sooner or later, and (2) he has a work for us to do. He does not need to give a specific reason; he knows what is in us. After all, Jesus knows what is "in man" (John 2:25).

Many criticize preaching about the wrath of God in order to win people to Christianity. But this criticism is unjustified. In fact, this type of preaching is God's idea. You may even say that motivating a lost sinner to be saved in order to avoid eternal punishment may be the best reason to become a Christian; this reason is clearly used by Jesus himself to warn us of the consequences of not believing in him. The most famous verse in the Bible, John 3:16—you may rightly call it the Bible in a nutshell—throws the warning of being eternally lost right in your face: those who believe will "not perish." I think a case can be made that in our present generation, when the preaching of hell has virtually disappeared from the church—but people still become Christians—many Christians today have a shallow view of Holy Scripture. I think this could be part of the reason.

Of course, people get genuinely converted to Christ without the preaching of hell. The conversion of the Ethiopian eunuch in Acts 8:26–39 is proof of this. So, too, is the admonition to wives and husbands to behave in a way that will win the spouse to the Lord (1 Cor. 7:12–16). These things said, it is still remarkable how many are converted nowadays by those who have a shallow view of Holy Scripture. God has always been merciful.

THREE PRINCIPLES TO REMEMBER ABOUT GOD'S CHASTENING

1. GOD'S CHASTENING IS INEVITABLE IF YOU ARE TRULY SAVED

God only chastens those who are truly his children. Truly born again. Saved. Justified by faith. "Whom the LORD *loves* He chastens" (Heb. 12:6 NKJV, emphasis mine). This is a proof that you are saved. "Chastening" is a word the New Testament uses exclusively for true children of God. "God is treating you as sons" when you are disciplined (v. 7). In fact, says the writer of Hebrews, if you are not disciplined, "then you are illegitimate children and not sons" (v. 8).

2. GOD'S CHASTENING IS PERFECT AND WISE

As parents, we do our best. We make mistakes. We can mess up terribly. I have punished my own children when they didn't deserve it. I have also overlooked their wrongs when I should have dealt with them. Additionally, I have punished them when I was angry (which is never good to do). I have punished them when looking over my shoulder in order to impress people looking on (which is an absolutely terrible thing to do). As the writer of Hebrews says, our earthly parents disciplined us "as it seemed best to them," but God does it entirely "for our good." Why? "That we may share his holiness" (v. 10). Thankfully, God never loses his temper when he disciplines us. He is never looking over his shoulder to see what the angels will think of the way he chastens us!

3. GOD'S DISCIPLINING OF US IS PAINFUL

Surprise, surprise—as if God needed to tell us—God's chastening is not pleasant. In a mastery of understatement, the writer of Hebrews says that God's chastening "seems painful rather than pleasant." But it accomplishes his purpose: "Later it yields the peaceful fruit of righteousness to those who have been trained by it" (v. 11). In a word: God's discipline works! Enforced learning.

King David is the best biblical illustration of God's painful chastening. Keep in mind that David was a man after God's own heart (1 Sam. 13:14). David had a heart that pursued God; God had a special fondness for David. I have been asked if God still regarded David as a man after his own heart after David's sin of adultery and murder. Answer: Yes; the way David responded to Nathan's stringent and painful declaration proves this. Furthermore, had this not been true after David's sin, the New Testament would not have repeated God's declaration in Acts 13:22. Not only that; the second part of David's life shows how much he loved God and how he demonstrated true godliness. He proved to be a better man than before.

In addition to the principles just listed, there are three kinds of chastening.

INTERNAL, EXTERNAL, AND TERMINAL CHASTENING

1. INTERNAL CHASTENING

This is God's plan A. Internal chastening happens when God operates on our hearts. It comes through preaching, teaching, a word of knowledge, or possibly a prophetic word. When the commander of the Lord's army spoke to Joshua, as we saw earlier, it was an example of internal chastening. Joshua was being taught a lesson about the nature of God. It was painful for him. He felt betrayed at first, then came to terms with what he needed to learn.

God speaks through preaching or a prophetic word when his two-edged sword cuts into our hearts and shows us our sin—or whatever we need to hear. This can be painful. God can expose our hearts in such a manner that we feel naked before the world—only to learn that he lovingly wants to teach us a lesson. When Josif Ton said to me, "R. T., you must totally forgive them. Until you totally forgive them, you will be in chains. Release them, and you will be released," these words cut to my heart. But they changed my life. "Faithful are the wounds of a friend" (Prov. 27:6).

God's plan A is the best way to have your problems solved. His plan A for Jonah was, "Go to Nineveh, that great city, and call out against it" (Jonah 1:2). God said, "Go"—but Jonah said, "No." Then God resorted to plan B.

2. EXTERNAL CHASTENING

Plan B comes into play because plan A didn't work. Thankfully, God did not give up on Jonah. Be thankful when God resorts to plan B—because he loves you and because he has work for you to do. With Jonah, God began to work behind the scenes. Jonah was now on board a ship heading for Tarshish. He thought he would enjoy a Mediterranean holiday, but God had other plans. He sent the wind. He sent the storm. He overruled the sailors' efforts to spare Jonah. The sailors finally threw Jonah overboard and the storm ceased. Meanwhile, Jonah was swallowed by a great fish. His prayer in chapter 2 reads like a psalm; God had gotten Jonah's attention. He doesn't compel us against our will, but he makes us willing to go. Jonah now prayed for strength to do the very thing he had been unwilling to do. Mercifully, God rescued Jonah and gave the same orders a second time: "Go to Nineveh" (3:2). God's plan did not change, but plan B changed Jonah.

Most of us need plan B sooner or later. Plan B may be when God puts us flat on our backs. It could be illness. It could be financial trouble. It may be the withholding of vindication. It may be the loss of a friend. There are a thousand options open to God when he decides to get our attention. For example, the people of Corinth wanted to know what was going on in their church. People were sickly and weak, and some were even dying. Paul answered: "So you want to know what is going on? This is 'why': you have abused the Lord's Supper—treating your poor brothers and sisters with contempt, serving the Lord's Supper before they can get to you from work." These believers were eating and drinking judgment on themselves (1 Cor. 11:29–30). God was trying to get their attention through external chastening combined with the internal chastening of Paul's word. Their sickness and weakness was part of their external chastening.

When Joseph and Mary went a day's journey without the child Jesus—but assumed he was with their party—Mary in particular seemed annoyed with her son after finding him: "Son, why have you treated us so?" (Luke 2:48). I think Mary was out of place. Mary thought she had a claim upon Jesus, but she too needed to see the glory of the Son of God. Even Mary, the mother of Jesus, had to come to terms with the truth that she must be willing to forsake any claim upon God.

3. Terminal Chastening

Terminal chastening is carried out when plan A and plan B fail. It is the sin unto death; the "sin that leads to death" (1 John 5:16). For example, some in Corinth had died (1 Cor. 11:30). Terminal chastening had happened to Ananias and Sapphira (Acts 5:1–10). It is also what happened to King Saul. He committed suicide, but God took the responsibility (1 Chron. 10:14; Hos. 13:11).

I can't be sure what needs to happen before God turns to terminal chastening. It likely comes after one blows away a second chance. God had given King Saul a second chance in 1 Samuel 15. Samuel had first pronounced chastisement upon Saul for his unlawful sacrifice in 1 Samuel 13:14. Then Saul completely lost his kingship when he would not obey God in fully destroying the Amalekites but thought his idea of sparing some of them was better (15:20–21). Had Jonah not obeyed when God came to him a "second time" (Jonah 3:1), he would almost certainly have faced the worst scenario for a believer—death. I believe I have known people like this in my own ministry. Terminal chastening occurs when God looks down from heaven and says, "Sorry, your time is up," and inflicts a premature death. I also believe terminal chastening is described in Hebrews 6:4–6 (when some believers fell away and could not be renewed again to repentance). Instead of taking them to heaven, God let them live. King Saul did live and go on wearing the crown for another twenty years after being rejected by God. I think Saul was an Old Testament example of Hebrews 6:4–6. Neither he nor those described in Hebrews 6:4–6 were able to experience being changed from glory to glory. Such people have no sense of being renewed to repentance. They are unreachable but still stay in the church. Sadly, there are many people like this in church today. They can be a nightmare to their leaders.

A THORN IN THE FLESH

When I teach about this topic, people always ask me about the Apostle Paul's thorn in the flesh. Was Paul's thorn in the flesh God's chastening?

Paul had received supernatural experiences from God. Not only did he have a spectacular conversion on the road to Damascus (Acts 9:1–9), but he also had unusual post-conversion experiences of the Holy Spirit. Not that Paul had done anything wrong; I think of these as a sort of "preventive medicine." Might God have deemed it necessary to give Paul compensatory disciplining? When someone has unusual talents, great gifts, or a high profile in God's kingdom, it can be easy for this person to take himself or herself a bit too seriously. Paul thus experienced what I would call *extreme chastening*—to keep him from being conceited, to keep him from taking himself too seriously, and possibly also to keep people around him from exalting him too much. He called it a "thorn" in his flesh (2 Cor. 12:7).

I reckon that Paul's thorn in the flesh was a forerunner for countless Christians. It seems that whereas all believers are given a measure of God's disciplining, not all have a thorn in the flesh. I suppose one could call the thorn a compliment—that God has entrusted it to such a high-profile person—but the pain from it punctures one's balloon. One way to know you have a thorn is if you pray again and again that it will go away and it does not leave. Paul said he prayed three times for his thorn to leave. God's answer to his prayer was that he would have a greater anointing (vv. 8–9).

Which would you prefer—less pain and less anointing? Or greater anointing but more pain? The greater the suffering, the greater the anointing. It is also true: the greater the anointing, the greater the suffering. All of us are prone to being conceited.

I have learned this much about God ever since he saved me at six years of age: he is very, very patient. The Bible says so (Ex. 34:6; Ps. 86:15). I can also tell you this categorically: I have experienced his patience firsthand. It is embarrassing to think of how patient God has been with me!

I often come to tears when I read Psalm 103:14: "For he knows our frame; he remembers that we are dust." Dr. Lloyd-Jones once told me he could not sing the following lines without weeping:

> Lead, Kindly Light, amid th'encircling gloom,
> Lead Thou me on!
> The night is dark, and I am far from home,
> Lead Thou me on!
> Keep Thou my feet; I do not ask to see
> The distant scene; one step enough for me.
>
> I was not ever thus, nor prayed that Thou
> Shouldst lead me on;
> I loved to choose and see my path; but now
> Lead Thou me on!
> I loved the garish day, and, spite of fears,
> Pride ruled my will. Remember not past years!
>
> —JOHN HENRY NEWMAN (1801–1890)

I must close this chapter by telling you, reader, that it is true I could not understand at the time why God would chasten me in August 1956. However, as I write this book sixty-six years later, I am amazed that God did not chasten me more since then. At the judgment seat of Christ you may well discover what God has tolerated in me in my lifetime. I think everything will be out in the open. I can only say that when Paul claimed to be the "chief" (KJV) or "foremost" of sinners (1 Tim. 1:15), I was not alive then.

CHAPTER 5

OUR INHERITANCE

❧

The lines have fallen for me in pleasant places;
indeed, I have a beautiful inheritance.
—PSALM 16:6

Enter into the promises of God. It is your inheritance. You
will do more in one year if you are really filled with the Holy
Ghost than you could do in fifty years apart from Him.
—SMITH WIGGLESWORTH (1859–1947)

O ur inheritance is God's reward for pleasing him. Inheritance, as I will show, is not the gift of salvation; rather, inheritance is offered to those who have *already accepted* the gift of salvation by transferring their trust in good works to the finished work of Jesus Christ. In other words, God gives you an inheritance when you please him *after* you are saved. All Christians are called to come into their inheritance. Some do, but some don't. Those who do will enjoy great blessing from God *on earth and* get a reward at the judgment seat of Christ. Those who don't come into their inheritance will live beneath their privilege as Christians on earth but will be saved by fire at the judgment seat of Christ.

In a few words: Inheritance is what you get by pleasing God.

As I mentioned in chapter 3, some Christians resent the idea of receiving a reward. I have run across believers in various parts of the world, perhaps most notably in Scotland, who feel that it is pious and honorable to disdain a reward. I once came across the following song in a Church of Scotland hymnal:

> My God, I love Thee; not because
> I hope for heaven thereby,
> Nor yet because who love Thee not
> Must die eternally.
>
> Then why, O blessed Jesus Christ,
> Should I not love Thee well?
> Not for the sake of winning heaven,
> Nor of escaping hell.
>
> Not with the hope of gaining aught,
> Not seeking a reward;
> But as Thyself hast loved me,
> O everlasting Lord!

These majestic words are attributed to St. Francis Xavier (1506–1552). Sincere though he may have been, not a single writer of the Bible, or anyone referred to in it, has ever come up to this standard. It is not what God expects of us. After all, "he remembers that we are dust" (Ps. 103:14).

No writer in the Bible encourages a standard so high that we outgrow the desire for a reward from God. Never forget: The concept of reward is God's idea. He made us. He knows how we are framed. Indeed, Jesus appeals to our wish for a *reward from God* when he challenged the Pharisees: "How can you believe, when you receive glory from one another and do not seek the glory that comes from the only God?" (John 5:44). The glory that comes from God is his rewarding us for eschewing the praise of people and desiring only his praise.

I believe that the kind of thinking which puts down the idea of God rewarding us is a subtle form of self-righteousness. This is not godliness but blindness. In my opinion, these people are trying to demonstrate, even if unwittingly, that "I am more holy than thou" by claiming that they supposedly worship God for his own sake and that a reward is beneath them. My reply to them is this: First, they are denying the way God made us. He knows our frame; he knows what you and I need in order to be motivated. Does he stoop to our weakness? Of course he does. Second, consider how God appealed to the two greatest men in the Old Testament. To Abraham, called the father of the faithful (Rom. 4:16), God promised:

> I will make of you a great nation, and I will bless you and make your name great, so that you will be a blessing. I will bless those who bless you, and him who dishonors you I will curse, and in you all the families of the earth shall be blessed. (Gen. 12:2–3)

> Your reward shall be very great. (15:1)

Moses was the greatest man and the greatest prophet in the Old Testament. Indeed, when summing up both the Old and New Testaments, two men stand out: Moses and Jesus.

For the law was given through Moses; grace and truth came through Jesus Christ. (John 1:17)

And what do you suppose motivated Moses to leave a life of luxury in the king's palace? Answer:

He considered the reproach of Christ greater wealth than the treasures of Egypt, for he was looking to the reward. (Heb. 11:26)

Here are words from Jesus:

And whoever gives one of these little ones even a cup of cold water because he is a disciple, truly, I say to you, he will by no means lose his reward. (Matt. 10:42)

Finally, even though tithing was commanded under the Mosaic law—people had to tithe whether they liked it or not—God nonetheless promised to reward those who obeyed!

Bring the full tithe into the storehouse, that there may be food in my house. And thereby put me to the test, says the Lord of hosts, if I will not open the windows of heaven for you and pour down for you a blessing until there is no more need. (Mal. 3:10)

FOUR RELEVANT WORDS

These four words may be used interchangeably: "reward" (Gr. *misthos*), "prize" (*brabeion*), "crown" (*stephanos*), and "inheritance" (*kleronomia*). In this chapter I will show you that these words refer mainly to the persons already saved. "Inheritance" as a noun or "to inherit" as a verb also refers to what is on offer to the saved. In Colossians 3:24 Paul uses both "inheritance" and "reward."

THE BIBLICAL ROOTS
FOR INHERITANCE

The origin of the teaching of inheritance goes back to Enoch, Noah, and Abraham. What they accomplished was done by *persistent faith*. *By faith* Enoch pleased God (Heb. 11:5). *By faith* Noah obeyed by building the ark (v. 7). *By faith* Abraham obeyed when he was "called to go out to a place that he was to receive as an *inheritance*" (v. 8, emphasis mine).

The New Testament generally refers to our *internal* inheritance, as we shall see in this chapter—what we may experience in our *hearts* by persistent faith. In Hebrews 11, however, the writer brings in examples of *external* inheritance: men and women in the Old Testament who experienced blessings in their *lives* due to their persistent faith.

MOSES AND THE
CHILDREN OF ISRAEL

Moses led the children of Israel out of Egypt so that they could inherit the land of Canaan, which flowed with milk and honey. This land belonged to Israel by promise. But that generation did not enter Canaan. They could have entered Canaan merely two years after being delivered from Pharoah. Caleb and Joshua had voted to conquer Canaan *right then*; but the other ten spies fearfully said, "We seemed to ourselves like grasshoppers" (Num. 13:33). Caleb and Joshua were outvoted because the majority lost heart; they gave in to unbelief. In a few words: The ancient people of Israel—except Joshua and Caleb—blew away their inheritance. This was when God swore in his wrath, "They shall not enter my rest" (Heb. 3:11). And they never did. They did try on their own to attempt to enter Canaan after God swore his oath—and failed (Num. 14:45).

When God swears an oath, one thing is crystal clear: it will never—ever—be changed. That entire generation of Israel—likely around two million men and women—died. Those all died who would not enter Canaan when they could have.

THE PURPOSE OF THE BOOK OF HEBREWS

The purpose of the epistle to the Hebrews was to urge Hebrew Christians to enter into their inheritance and not repeat the error of their ancestors who had forfeited their inheritance. As stated earlier: all Christians are called to come into their inheritance; some do, some don't. The writer of Hebrews likens Christian Jews of the first century to the generation of Moses some 1300 years before. He warns them (Heb. 6:4–6). He encourages them (6:9ff; 10:35ff). He reminds them in detail of what happened when God swore an oath regarding those Israelites who doubted God and did not accept the offer to enter the Promised Land.

For who were those who heard and yet rebelled? Was it not all those who left Egypt led by Moses? And with whom was he provoked for forty years? Was it not with those who sinned, whose bodies fell in the wilderness? And to whom did he swear that they would not enter his rest, but to those who were disobedient? So we see that they were unable to enter because of unbelief. (Heb. 3:16–19)

How the Nature and Details of Our Inheritance Are Determined

God chose the inheritance of the next generation of Israelites. You could call it the Joshua generation. The details of their inheritance were out of their hands. First, God chose Joshua to succeed Moses. But Moses was able to outline what the new generation under Joshua should expect once they entered the land of Canaan. There were twelve tribes of Israel. Where each tribe should reside would not be determined by a vote—God would decide. Joshua would cast lots. All the tribes had no say in where they would live.

Moses put it this way:

You shall inherit the land by lot according to your clans. To a large tribe you shall give a large inheritance, and to a small tribe you shall give a small inheritance. Wherever the lot falls for anyone, that shall be his. (Num. 33:54)

Lots were cast to avoid rivalry, jealousy, or a possibility that a tribal leader would accuse Moses or Joshua of playing favorites.

Those from Judah might have said, "We want to reside in the northern part of Canaan." And the tribe of Benjamin might have said, "Put us over here—where the weather is warmer." But God took the responsibility. As the psalmist put it, "He chose our inheritance for us" (Ps. 47:4 NIV). It was out of Joshua's hands. It was out of Moses's hands. It was out of the hands of anyone among the children of Israel. God would decide.

It was not easy for the generation of Joshua to come into their inheritance. It was a hard fight—to the end. But they did it:

> So Joshua took the whole land, according to all that the Lord had spoken to Moses. And Joshua gave it for an inheritance to Israel according to their tribal allotments. And the land had rest from war. (Josh. 11:23)

This laborious process of coming into our inheritance is true of you and me, too—to this day. It can be very humbling. But that's the way it is.

The writer of Hebrews uses different words to describe the Christian's inheritance. It could be called "the rest" that remains for God's people (Heb. 4:9). Indeed, as the promised land had "rest from war," so too those who have entered into God's rest have "also rested from [their] works as God did from his" (v. 10). Inheritance can be also called "full assurance" (6:11; 10:22). This assurance would consist in experiencing God's *swearing of an oath to us* (6:17–19). In receiving assurance through this oath, we embrace the promise of entering into God's rest (10:36ff). The writer gives his readers encouragement: "The promise of entering his rest *still stands*" (4:1, emphasis mine). This means these Hebrew believers have not—at least so far—crossed over the line whereby God would swear in his wrath as he did against ancient Israel.

How does the writer know this? He is writing under the inspiration of the Holy Spirit. He is persuaded of "better things" for them: "things that belong to salvation" (6:9). He knows that these Hebrews are saved. Likewise, Canaan did belong to ancient Israel in Moses's day. These people were also saved—but the generation in the wilderness forfeited their inheritance of Canaan. In the same way, inheritance "belongs" to these Hebrews in the first century because it accompanies salvation. It is potentially theirs. But as the children of Israel had to fight for their territory in Canaan, the writer to the Hebrews says that his readers must "strive" (Gr. *spoudasomen*—"be diligent"; "labor," KJV) to enter into that rest (4:11). It "accompanies salvation" (Gr. *echomena soterias*). In a few words: Just as Canaan belonged to ancient Israel—who blew it away—the writer shows a scary parallel as to what it would be like if God swore an oath in wrath against these first century Hebrews:

> For it is impossible, in the case of those who have once been enlightened, who have tasted the heavenly gift, and have shared in the Holy Spirit, and have tasted the goodness of the word of God and the powers of the age to come, and then have fallen away, to restore them again to repentance. (6:4–6)

The people described in Hebrews 6:4–6 are saved. The writer bends over backward to demonstrate this by using terms that apply to those born again: "enlightened," "shared in the Holy Spirit," "tasted of the powers of the age to come," etc. I have heard some counter that they only tasted, and that one can taste without swallowing. But the same word is used in Hebrews 2:9—that Jesus would "taste" death for everyone. Did Jesus only taste death but did not die? Of course he died! Moreover, Hebrews 6:6 says they could not be restored "again" (Gr. *palin*—"again"). That such could not be renewed "again" to repentance shows that they had indeed formerly repented and trusted in Christ.

Some readers may know that Hebrews 6:4–6 has been a theological battleground for Calvinists (who traditionally believe that saved people cannot fall away) and Arminians (who believe that saved people can fall away and therefore lose their salvation). Both Calvinists and Arminians are uncomfortable with this passage. Calvinists, in order to make things fit into their theological paradigm, tend to show that those described were not truly saved but only appeared to be saved. Arminians are disturbed because they hold that those who fall away can be restored, but these verses clearly show that one cannot be restored!

I am not fence-straddling by my interpretation of Hebrews 6:4–6. I believe these words mean exactly what they say. The writer of Hebrews does not say these people lose their salvation; the writer says that they cannot be renewed "again" to *repentance*. When God withdraws the privilege of repentance, it means these people cannot hear God speak; they cannot ever again enjoy being changed from "glory to glory" (2 Cor. 3:18 KJV). Being changed from glory to glory is a way of describing one's internal inheritance.

I have gone into this detail because I too once held to the Reformed view that these people were illuminated but not regenerated. It is hard to give up one's cherished views—this took me years. But in the end exegetical integrity demanded that I humbly admit to the obvious truth. It is a little bit embarrassing to have to change a view after having taken a stand for so long! But I had to admit that the writer of Hebrews could not have used stronger words to prove that these people were truly saved. The children of Israel were not only converted; they had "tasted the heavenly gift"! They had "shared in the Holy Spirit"! They had seen "the powers of the age to come" (Heb. 6:4, 5)! As for the ancient children of Israel, they had not only experienced Passover and the crossing of the Red Sea, but had eaten the manna in the desert and seen God powerfully at work. But they still forfeited their inheritance. Thankfully, we will still see these children of Israel in heaven.

Could these Hebrew Christians lose their salvation? No, thank God. But they were in danger of becoming stone-deaf to the Holy Spirit. Ancient Israel, whom God swore against in wrath, could no longer hear God's voice. This is why we have the words, "If you hear his voice" (3:7). The author quotes Psalm 95 because these first-century Hebrew Christians had already become "dull of hearing" (5:11).

The implied warning is: *Do not become stone-deaf.* I would lovingly say to the reader: Be sure that you too can always hear God speak; that you are sensitive to the voice of the Spirit. Be thankful when you can *sense*—feel it—when you have grieved the Spirit, so that you can quickly close the time gap between sin and repentance. Indeed, be thankful when you are keen to repent anytime you err. This is a good sign that you are hearing God speak.

At the natural level, some people become deaf by an accident. What a terrible thing to happen! My wife Louise once punctured her eardrum and lost hearing in one ear for a while. (This led her to learn sign language. We consequentially had a wonderful ministry to the deaf at Westminster Chapel—a beautiful example of Romans 8:28.) However, most people who become deaf do so gradually. That is not a happy thing to experience, either. I am currently losing my hearing. The first sign of deafness in my case was when I found myself cupping my hand over my ear to hear better. It works—but it's only a matter of time before I will need a hearing aid. Then, in some cases, one later needs a stronger hearing aid. Then an even stronger one. The worst scenario is when one becomes "profoundly deaf"—as it is often put in the deaf world. It is often called being *stone-deaf*—when one hears *nothing*. I would hate for this to happen to me. But I would prefer to be stone-deaf at the natural level than at the spiritual level. May God grant that you or I never become stone-deaf to the Holy Spirit. You can find my exposition of Hebrews 6 in my book, *Are You Stone Deaf to the Spirit or Rediscovering God?*

At the spiritual level, apparently, one can lose hearing God's voice gradually. These Hebrew Christians were already becoming "dull of hearing" (Heb. 5:11). The worst scenario would be to become stone-deaf—which is the condition described in Hebrews 6:4–6. At this point one cannot hear God speak at all. This is why these people cannot be renewed to repentance.

When we get to heaven, we will learn whether these first-century Christian Jews, whom the author of the epistle to the Hebrews wrote to, eventually came into their inheritance. The same would be true concerning the Gentile Galatians—Paul was very worried about them. But they were saved; otherwise, Paul would not have pleaded with them as he did (e.g., Gal. 4:19; 5:16–26). The teaching on Christians coming into their inheritance may be found in most of Paul's letters, especially in Romans 4. Once you grasp this teaching, you will find that it is implicit in nearly all the books of the New Testament.

INHERITANCE AND ENTERING THE KINGDOM OF GOD

One must be born again to enter the kingdom of God (John 3:3–8). It is a sovereign work of the Holy Spirit (v. 8). However, being born again does not mean that you "automatically" enter into your inheritance. Paul and Barnabas proved this by reminding their disciples that "through many tribulations [hardships] we must *enter the kingdom of God*" (Acts 14:22, emphasis mine). As Jesus taught, entering the kingdom of God requires the righteousness that *surpasses* that of the Pharisees (Matt. 5:20)! You may recall that the kingdom of God is *the realm of the ungrieved Spirit*. Acts 14:22 does not describe how you get saved, as if salvation comes by going through tribulation or hardship. It means that entering the kingdom of God is the same as entering into God's *rest* by striving, or laboring (Heb. 4:11—"mak[ing] every effort," NIV). You do not "do your best" to be born again; it is a work of the Spirit which you are passive under. But you *do* do your best when entering the kingdom of God as described in Acts 14:22. This also explains why Jesus said "only with difficulty will a rich person enter the kingdom of heaven . . . it is easier for a camel to go through the eye of a needle than for a rich person to enter the kingdom of God" (Matt. 19:23–24). This is not how a person is born again, but how one with effort and hardship enters the kingdom of God.

There is, therefore, a definite demarcation between being justified by faith (saved, born again, regeneration) and entering the kingdom of God as Jesus described it in the Sermon on the Mount (Matt. 5:20). Jesus indeed said to Nicodemus that you cannot enter the kingdom apart from being born again (John 3:3). You cannot enter it without being justified by faith in the blood of Jesus

(Rom. 5:9). But to grasp what Jesus fully means by "kingdom of God" may require some readers to shift gears theologically if one thinks that every saved person comes into his or her inheritance automatically by being born of the Spirit.

Entering the kingdom of God through much tribulation, then, describes the effort required by all of us. You may also call it entering into God's rest.

A helpful way to see the two uses of "kingdom of God" in John 3:3 and Acts 14:22—and other uses of this term in the New Testament—is this: they might be seen as a circle within a circle. Picture this: A big circle of brightness that one enters when born again. Outside the circle is darkness. But one passes from darkness into light when born again. Then picture a smaller circle of brilliant brightness inside the larger circle. We enter the smaller circle of brilliant brightness through hardship. Through effort. Resisting temptation. Refusing to lust. Struggling. Avoiding grieving the Spirit. Practicing total forgiveness. Dignifying our trials. Controlling our tongues. This isn't always easy.

Persistent faith is required to come into one's inheritance. As I keep saying: some do, some don't. There are people who think that those who don't enter their inheritance—and live on the straight and narrow all the time—were never converted in the first place. I do not accept that theory. I believe there are people—many, if the truth be known—who have had a genuine conversion but later backslide or lose heart for some reason. For example, Paul instructed the Corinthians that even the soul of the man who slept with his father's wife would be saved through the destruction of the flesh (1 Cor. 5:5). You see, Paul does not say this man has no hope or is eternally lost. I have seen extreme situations like this one from Corinth countless times as a pastor. My point is this:

severe backsliding does not necessarily mean that a person wasn't truly converted.

The Greek word for inheritance is *kleronomia*. You don't need to know Greek to understand what I am teaching; I spell it out so that you can easily recognize the similarity of the words. For instance, Paul encouraged bondservants to be faithful to their earthly masters, working "heartily, as for the Lord and not for men, knowing that from the Lord you will receive the inheritance [*kleronomia*] as your reward" (Col. 3:23–24). Paul consistently uses the verb *kleronomeo* and the noun *kleronomia* in his letters to the Corinthians, the Galatians, and the Ephesians:

> Or do you not know that the unrighteous will not inherit [Gr. *kleronomesousin*] the kingdom of God? Do not be deceived: neither the sexually immoral, nor idolators, nor adulterers, nor men who practice homosexuality, nor thieves, nor the greedy, nor drunkards, nor revilers, nor swindlers will inherit [Gr. *kleronomesousin*] the kingdom of God. And such were some of you. But you were washed, you were sanctified, you were justified in the name of the Lord Jesus Christ and by the Spirit of our God. (1 Cor. 6:9–11)

The clear teaching of this passage is a warning for the Corinthians to resist slipping back into their pre-conversion life or face forfeiture of their inheritance in the kingdom.

To the Galatians, Paul says the same thing:

> Now the works of the flesh are evident: sexual immorality, impurity, sensuality, idolatry, sorcery, enmity, strife, jealousy, fits of anger, rivalries, dissensions, divisions, envy,

drunkenness, orgies, and things like these. I warn you, as I
warned you before, that those who do such things will not
inherit [Gr. *kleronomesousin*] the kingdom of God. (Gal. 5:19–21)

Why does Paul write like this? Because he knows that these
converted Gentiles could lose their inheritance in the kingdom
of God if they revert to their past life. He knows they have been
saved (see Galatians 3:2; 4:6; 5:7). His chief concern at that time was
that they might become trapped under the burden of the Mosaic
law, which would equally cause them to forfeit their inheritance.

Likewise, Paul's warning to the Ephesians seeks to keep that
church focused on securing its inheritance:

But sexual immorality and all impurity or covetousness must
not even be named among you, as is proper among saints. Let
there be no filthiness nor foolish talk nor crude joking, which
are out of place, but instead let there be thanksgiving. For you
may be sure of this, that everyone who is sexually immoral or
impure, or who is covetous (that is, an idolater), has no inheritance [Gr. *kleronomian*] in the kingdom of Christ and God.
(Eph. 5:3–5)

INTERNAL AND EXTERNAL INHERITANCE

Now I need to explain more about inheritance because there are
two ways to understand inheritance: internally and externally.

Internal inheritance refers to God's dealing with us at the spiritual level. Paul believed the sealing—or filling—of the Spirit

came "after" one believed (1:13 KJV). For some it comes at conversion—as in the case of Cornelius in Acts 10. But more often than not, this sealing seems to follow one's conversion. And yet as the early church had virtually a second Pentecost in Acts 4:31, when the place was "shaken" and they were all "filled with the Holy Spirit," so too a Christian may have continued fillings of the Spirit.

Paul prayed this for the Ephesians:

Having the eyes of your hearts enlightened, that you may know what is the hope to which he has called you, what are the riches of his glorious inheritance in the saints, and what is the immeasurable greatness of his power toward us who believe, according to the working of his great might that he worked in Christ. (Eph. 1:18–20)

He also instructed the Ephesians, "Be filled with the Spirit" (5:18), although they already had the Holy Spirit. This is what Paul calls being changed "from one degree of glory to another. For this comes from the Lord who is the Spirit" (2 Cor. 3:18). I think of the words of Smith Wigglesworth: "Enter into the promises of God. It is your inheritance. You will do more in one year if you are really filled with the Holy Ghost than you could do in fifty years apart from Him."

The way forward to enjoy a rich internal inheritance is to walk in the light, as in 1 John 1:7: "If we walk in the light, as he is in the light, we have fellowship with one another, and the blood of Jesus his Son cleanses us from all sin." We cannot deny that in the church some Christians grow faster than others; some read their Bible more than others; some are apparently more spiritual than others; some spend more time alone with God than others; some want to be more involved in the work of the Lord than others; and some enjoy attending Bible studies more than others. These things pertain to one's internal inheritance.

Your internal inheritance will be very important to you at the judgment seat of Christ. One's external inheritance may seem more important now. But our reward at the judgment seat of Christ will center on our internal inheritance: what kind of husband I have been, what kind of father I was, and whether I have practiced what I preach on total forgiveness, dignifying the trial, and walking in the light.

External inheritance largely refers to the way God uses your *natural* gifts in his kingdom. When David said, "I have a beautiful inheritance" because "the lines have fallen for me in pleasant places" (Ps. 16:6), he was referring to the way God had blessed him. He was chosen to be king (1 Sam. 16:12). He killed the giant Goliath (17:49–51). He was a gifted musician (16:18). He was also a most successful king. One could say that being a man after God's own heart explains David's many gifts—but I think this refers to his love for God. In any case, God chose David's inheritance for him (Ps. 47:4). When he declares the lines have "fallen" to him, this was his way of saying, "It is what God did." As the casting of lots lay behind the tribes of Israel's inheritance, so David knew that what had happened to him was out of his hands.

In comparison to David, your external inheritance refers mostly to God's plans for your life—your calling in life. Are you a teacher? Are you gifted in sports? Are you intellectual? Do you like to read books? Do you prefer science to arts? Would you enjoy being a nurse? Are you a physician? Did you do well in school? Do you like computers? Are you a waiter or waitress?

Do you work in a repair shop? Are your natural gifts useful in church work?

Many people will first ask, "What is my external inheritance?" I answer: Don't ask, "What is my external inheritance?" Ask, "What is my internal inheritance?" Ask whether your chief concern is a love for God. Do I want to please him? Am I walking in the light? Do I keep my eyes on Jesus? How much do I pray?

Also consider your own place in the body of Christ. In 1 Corinthians 12 Paul refers to both spiritual gifts (vv. 4–11) and our usefulness in the body of Christ. There are those who have high profiles: they are the eyes, the ears, or the head. Some have a low profile in the body: they are called "unpresentable parts" (12:23) which cannot be seen—your intestines, kidneys, pancreas. Your spiritual inheritance will be determined partly by whether you *graciously accept your place* in the body. Are you jealous because you are not the head? Do you feel cheated if you are never noticed? Paul makes the case that *all* the parts of the body are needed. You cannot live without a pancreas, and somebody is needed to do things that get no attention. Are you okay with that? Or do you murmur and complain because your only job is to sweep floors?

What if your gift is that of "helps" (12:28 KJV) or "helping"? This gift may not appeal to one's ego, but if we accept our gift—or "measure of faith" (Rom. 12:3)—this pleases God. If we realize that our reward at the judgment seat of Christ will be in proportion to our faithfulness in what is least (Luke 16:10)—and not in what gets greatly noticed by people—this may serve to motivate us to be faithful in small things.

As we will see further in the next chapter, your reward in

heaven will be largely determined by *how you accept your place* in the body of Christ now.

But this much we can know for sure: Hebrews 11 describes what people did by persistent faith to secure their inheritance. With all those men and women described—whether Jacob, Moses, Sarah, Samuel, Barak, or Jephthah—their abiding faith explained their exploits. In other words, their internal inheritance came before their external inheritance was realized. It was their *faith*. Their persistent faith. Their not giving up believing God. The writer shows what happens to those who discover how God rewards those who diligently seek him (v. 6). I used to say to the members of Westminster Chapel: "Why can't *all of us* be like those described in Hebrews 11?" These were ordinary people who ended up doing extraordinary things because of their persistent faith. They became famous because of their faith. Their place in history was assured by their faith, not by their intelligence—or education—or connections. Yes, some of them showed skill in their natural gifts. But they would never—ever—have been known apart from their personal diligent faith. Their internal inheritance lay behind their successes and fame.

You may ask this question: what is the connection between spiritual gifts that make up the body of Christ and those who had persistent faith in Hebrews 11? First, it is our *faithfulness* to what God has given us that matters most. Paul urged that we accept the "measure," or limit, of our faith in Romans 12:3. We must not promote ourselves to the level of our incompetence. God will not do that. This means we need to accept what God has given us. One's gift may seem insignificant because it is not greatly or widely recognized—like the gift of "helps." However, God is pleased by our faithfulness—faithfulness in the small things, as in

Luke 16:10. Second, those who turned their worlds upside down in Hebrews 11 did so by *believing God's promises* and not giving up, even if this meant going against conventional wisdom. Noah built an ark—an unprecedented feat (v. 7). Abraham obeyed the Lord but did not know for a good while where he was going (v. 8). All those who are listed in Hebrews 11 trusted God in doing what he had commanded them to do or in waiting for him to fulfill what he had promised to do. Those in Hebrews 11 undoubtedly had gifts. Moses had a gift of leadership, but he would not have excelled in that gift had he not first left the palace of Pharaoh; this took faith (v. 24).

These things said, God has shown how he can overrule the general principles I have outlined. Moses committed murder, and yet he became the one who gave us the Ten Commandments that includes: "You shall not murder" (Ex. 20:13). David committed adultery and murder, but God forgave him and continued to use him. David's sin even seems far worse than Saul's! But God used David and rejected Saul. He is sovereign and does what he pleases.

God has called all believers to come into their inheritance. Some do, and some don't. I am a Bible teacher. That is my external inheritance. I could not have known fifty years ago that I would one day have an international ministry. Yes, I did have a vision of this. But had I gotten completely off the rails—whether with sex or money—I would not have had the ministry I have now. Accordingly, one's external inheritance and internal inheritance— our obedience to God—are intertwined.

Therefore, I am totally convinced of this: our internal inheritance will be what matters at the judgment seat of Christ. We turn to this subject now.

CHAPTER 6

THE JUDGMENT
SEAT OF CHRIST

*It is appointed for man to die once, and after that comes
judgment.*

— HEBREWS 9:27

*For we must all appear before the judgment seat of Christ, so
that each one may receive what is due for what he has done
in the body, whether good or evil.*

— 2 CORINTHIANS 5:10

*There are only two days on my calendar. Today and the day
of judgment.*

— MARTIN LUTHER (1483–1546)

A s I mentioned in chapter 1, Martin Luther once said he expects three surprises when he gets to heaven. First, there will be people there whom he didn't think would be there. Second, there will be people missing whom he thought would be there. Third, "that I am there myself." If I may paraphrase Luther, I expect three surprises at the judgment seat of Christ. First, there will be those who get a reward whom I thought would be saved by fire and not get a reward. Second, there will be those saved by fire whom I thought would certainly receive a reward. Third, that I myself am not saved by fire but receive a reward.

One thing is certain: a final judgment awaits every single one of us. The last verses of Ecclesiastes make this point:

> The end of the matter; all has been heard. Fear God and keep his commandments, for this is the whole duty of man. For God will bring every deed into judgment, with every secret thing, whether good or evil. (Eccl. 12:13–14)

God will have the last word—righteousness will be vindicated. In the meantime, evil appears to be unlimited all over the world. The psalmist David said that God has "put all things under his feet" (Ps. 8:6). This is quoted in Hebrews 2:8, which adds, making the obvious point, *"At present, we do not yet see everything in subjection to him"* (emphasis mine). Quite. Then comes the glorious observation by the writer of Hebrews: We see Jesus!

> But we see him who for a little while was made lower than the angels, namely Jesus, crowned with glory and honor because of the suffering of death, so that by the grace of God he might taste death for everyone. (v. 9)

Yes: "But we see Jesus." Jesus. Even as we face judgment, this is our hope. That is the basis for this chapter. What hope have we that God will have the last word? One answer: Jesus.

Why Does God Allow Suffering?

We started the Pilot Light ministry at Westminster Chapel in May 1982. For my final twenty years at Westminster I was out on the street of Buckingham Gate every Saturday talking to strangers. To passersby. To tourists. To members of Parliament. There I found out firsthand what I already knew: the chief reason people give for not believing in God is, "Why is there evil and suffering in the world?" Some suppose they are the first to think this thought!

But the Old Testament prophet Habakkuk saw this thousands of years ago. Habakkuk felt betrayed by God. He not only allowed suffering and injustice but even appeared to side with Israel's enemy. Habakkuk wanted to know *why*. Yes. Habakkuk wanted to know what we all want to know: "Why, why, why, Lord, do you allow evil and suffering?"

God replied in so many words: "OK, Habakkuk, meet me at the watchpost and station yourself on the tower." Habakkuk was excited. He was at last going to discover what God himself would say about the problem of evil. "I will take my stand at my watchpost and station myself on the tower, and look out to see what he will say to me, and what I will answer concerning my complaint," Habakkuk declared (Hab. 2:1). Then came the Lord's answer. His answer was so important that part of it gets used in the New Testament three times. I am sure you will notice which part.

Write the vision;
>   make it plain on tablets,
>   so he may run who reads it.
> For still the vision awaits its appointed time;
>   it hastens to the end—it will not lie.
> If it seems slow, wait for it;
>   it will surely come; it will not delay.

> Behold, his soul is puffed up; it is not upright
>   within him,
>   but the righteous shall live by his faith. (2:2–4)

Habakkuk was disappointed by God's response: wait a little longer. Wouldn't we all be? It seemed that God was kicking the can down the road. The vision refers to "the end"—whatever does this mean? It means what it says—the "end." The last day. The very last day. The final judgment. At that time God will explain why he has allowed suffering—but not before.

The final phrase in Hebrew is best interpreted: "the righteous [the just] shall live by my faithfulness"—that is, live by the faithfulness of God. In the New Testament, Habakkuk 2:4 is quoted three times—in Romans 1:17, Galatians 3:11, and Hebrews 10:38. In Romans and Galatians, Paul uses this quotation to support the teaching of justification by faith alone. In Hebrews 10:38, however, it mirrors the original meaning: living by the faithfulness of God to keep his word. The meaning of Habakkuk 2:4 is that righteousness will be imputed to the person who is willing to wait until the end! In other words, if you will live by the faithfulness of God; if you will trust his word;

and if you are willing to wait until the last day for God to clear his name and reveal why he has allowed evil to flourish, God imputes righteousness to you!

Disappointed though Habakkuk was, he accepted God's verdict. Habakkuk might have said, "That's not fair, Lord." He might also have said, "That's not good enough. I want the answer to the problem of evil now—right now." But Habakkuk made the decision to wait. How do we know? Listen to him:

> Though the fig tree should not blossom,
>> nor fruit be on the vines,
> the produce of the olive fail
>> and the fields yield no food,
> the flock be cut off from the fold
>> and there be no herd in the stalls,
> yet I will rejoice in the LORD;
>> I will take joy in the God of my salvation.
> GOD, the Lord, is my strength;
>> he makes my feet like the deer's;
>> he makes me tread on my high places. (3:17–19)

WHAT ABOUT US?

What hope do I have that what I write in this chapter is true? What hope do you have that there will be a last day, a day of days, when Jesus Christ himself reveals his glory and power? The only answer is this: The Bible is true.

That said, what I know about the final judgment is that the

New Testament refers to it in these terms: "the day of judgment" (Matt. 11:24; 2 Pet. 2:9; 1 John 4:17); "the judgment seat of God" (Rom. 14:10); "the judgment seat of Christ" (2 Cor. 5:10); "[the] judgment" (Heb. 9:27); "the judgment of the great day" (Jude 6); and "a great white throne" (Rev. 20:11).

Some still say, "If there is a God, he has a lot to answer for." The most hated, the most maligned, the most accused, and yet faultless person is God Almighty. The Father of Jesus. The first person of the Trinity.

Judgment day will be the scariest day of all time. It will be the first time ever in the history of humankind that true, fair, and pure justice is manifested. The Supreme Court that resides in Washington, D.C. has left many a person feeling bewildered and betrayed by its faulty judgments. But even the Supreme Court will bow before the great white throne. This will be the last word, indeed. There will be no further appeal. I can safely predict that when the Righteous Judge clears his name, all people will be left staggered, stunned, and silenced. The most ingenious, the most brilliant, and the most revered minds of all time will say, "Why didn't we think of this?" The reason: Judgment is hidden. It is hidden so that we might be given the privilege of faith. If God had brought judgment day forward, no person would need faith. All the world will *wail* when Jesus appears in the clouds (Rev. 1:7) because faith is no longer possible. All will see. All will "believe"— but it won't be faith at work. Faith is when we believe without seeing (Heb. 11:1). And all will *see* on that day.

The greatest suffering and evil in the history of the universe was the crucifixion of Jesus. There was nothing fair about it—Jesus did not even get a fair trial. Jews and Romans did this because they hated Jesus, who was wholly righteous. And yet God allowed this gross injustice to happen. Why? Maybe God will explain the cause of evil at the judgment. This will be when God clears his name. How will he do it? Habakkuk 2:1–4 promised that he would do it in the end—the last day. But no sooner. Those who say, "I won't wait that long" will forfeit the promise that goes to those who will trust God's faithfulness (v. 4). When God reveals his reason for allowing suffering, the brightest minds will say, "I hadn't thought of that." Indeed. They could not think of it because it is hidden. But God will reveal his wisdom and integrity on the last day.

When God reveals the reason for suffering, extreme distraught, deepest woe, incalculable sorrow, and indescribable desperation will follow. No language, no vocabulary, and no pictures would even come close to show in advance what it will be like on that day. The smug confidence of unbelief—the defense mechanism self-righteous people have used in their comfortable hatred toward the Most High God—will evaporate faster than a thousand suns would cause a drop of water to disappear.

More than once Jesus said this sort of thing:

For nothing is covered that will not be revealed, or hidden that will not be known. (Matt. 10:26)

For nothing is hidden except to be made manifest; nor is anything secret except to come to light. (Mark 4:22)

For nothing is hidden that will not be made manifest, nor is anything secret that will not be known and come to light. (Luke 8:17)

Nothing is covered up that will not be revealed, or hidden that will not be known. Therefore whatever you have said in the dark shall be heard in the light, and what you have whispered in private rooms shall be proclaimed on the housetops. (12:2–3)

It is not certain whether all of these statements refer to the final judgment day. But language like this shows that we are not our own and the privacy we so often guard may be withdrawn from us one day. It is also uncertain whether *all* secrets of *all* people—saved and lost—will be revealed.

WHAT SINS WILL BE REVEALED?

There are basically two views as to whether saved people's secrets will be revealed. First, the predominant view among Christians is that our sins are covered by the blood of Christ; that they have been buried in the "sea of forgetfulness." As the prophet Micah declared:

You will cast all our sins
into the depths of the sea. (Mic. 7:19)

The Apostle Paul said that God would forgive our sins; that they are "covered" (Rom. 4:7). The blood of Jesus covers them. Finally, King David said that "as far as the east is from the west, so far does he remove our transgressions from us" (Ps. 103:12).

But why does Paul say to Christians, "We [a reference to himself and all Christians] must all appear before the judgment seat of Christ, so that each one may receive what is due for what he has done in the body, whether good or evil" (2 Cor. 5:10)? If our sins have been covered—hidden—by the blood of Christ, how can Paul say we will give an account for the deeds done in the body?

My friend Arthur Blessitt takes the view that our whole lives will be exposed at the judgment. He asks: Why should the sins of the people in the Bible—like Samson or King David—be openly revealed but all the rest of us not have our whole lives exposed? Why should we get a free pass (so to speak)?

I will return to this issue in a minute.

My least favorite verses in the Bible contain some scary words, such as these:

> I tell you, on the day of judgment people will give account for every careless word they speak, for by your words you will be justified, and by your words you will be condemned. (Matt. 12:36–37)

However, the Apostle Paul did take great comfort from the coming judgment seat of Christ when people were accusing him:

> But with me it is a very small thing that I should be judged by you or by any human court. In fact, I do not even judge myself. For I am not aware of anything against myself, but I am not thereby acquitted. It is the Lord who judges me. Therefore do not pronounce judgment before the time, before the Lord comes, who will bring to light the things now hidden in darkness and will disclose the purposes of the heart. Then each one will receive his commendation from God. (1 Cor. 4:3–5)

This isn't the only place where Paul shows his clear perception of the judgment seat of Christ. In Romans 14:10 he said that "we will all stand before the judgment seat of *God*" (emphasis mine). In both Romans 14:10 and 2 Corinthians 5:10 he uses the Greek word *bema*, which is translated as "judgment." I have been to the historic Bema Seat in Corinth twice. It was where awards were given out, but also where criminals were sentenced. Everything was out in the open for all to see. Paul used this word because every person in the Gentile world would have understood the meaning of *bema*.

WHERE DID THE TEACHING ABOUT THE FINAL JUDGMENT COME FROM?

It is impossible to know exactly when, where, or by whom the teaching of a final judgment was first uttered. Isaiah put it like this:

> Enter into the rock
>> and hide in the dust
> from before the terror of the LORD,
>> and from the splendor of his majesty.
> The haughty looks of man shall be brought low,
>> and the lofty pride of men shall be humbled,
> and the LORD alone will be exalted in that day.
>> (Isa. 2:10–11)

"That day" would seem to be the final day of judgment. But I cannot say for sure. The prophet Joel, however, did proclaim a coming "day." This could refer to a day that would come in Joel's generation—when God stepped in to judge. But it also could be a reference to the final day.

> Blow a trumpet in Zion;
>> sound an alarm on my holy mountain!
> Let all the inhabitants of the land tremble,
>> for the day of the LORD is coming; it is near,
> a day of darkness and gloom,
>> a day of clouds and thick darkness! . . .
> For the day of the LORD is great and very awesome;
>> who can endure it? (Joel 2:1–2, 11)

What we know for sure is that when Jesus spoke of "that day" in his Sermon on the Mount, he assumed that all his hearers knew what he was talking about:

> On that day many will say to me, "Lord, Lord, did we not prophesy in your name, and cast out demons in your name, and do many mighty works in your name?" And then will I declare to them, "I never knew you; depart from me, you workers of lawlessness." (Matt. 7:22–23)

It should be noted that Jesus said, "Many will say to *me* . . . then will *I* declare to them" (emphasis mine). This shows that Jesus himself will be the Judge! Indeed, Paul preached at the Areopagus in Athens that the Final Judge would be Jesus:

> He [God] has fixed a day on which he will judge the world in righteousness by a man whom he has appointed; and of this

he has given assurance to all by raising him from the dead.
(Acts 17:31)

Paul also said in another place that Jesus would be the Judge:

I charge you in the presence of God and of Christ Jesus, who is
to judge the living and the dead, and by his appearing and his
kingdom. (2 Tim. 4:1)

VINDICATION

The one word—call it the common denominator—that explains,
underlines, and prevails throughout the judgment seat of Christ
is this: vindication. This means to be cleared from blame or suspi-
cion. Vindication is proof that one has got it right and is justified.
The truth about everything and everybody will be out in the open.
I am sure of this: the *truth* will be vindicated. God is no respecter
of persons. He will not clear my name because he likes me or
because I have been in the ministry a long while—or because
you have been a good Christian. As God showed no partiality
when stepping in to judge Moses or David—but only vindicated
truth—so pure justice will be meted out on that day of days. This
is partly why judgment day will be the scariest day of one's life.
When John said that some could have "boldness" (KJV) or "confidence" on the day of judgment (1 John 4:17), I can understand if
this means knowing in advance whether I will go to heaven or
hell. I am sure I will go to heaven. But if this means boldness with
regard to my personal life and feeling guaranteed of receiving a
reward, I can only say that I don't have such assurance!

Things I Am Sure Of

Although there are mysteries about the order and nature of the judgment seat of Christ, I am sure of five things.

The Bible Will Be Vindicated

The very occasion of the judgment seat of Christ will speak for itself. The dead being raised would seem to settle the truth of the Bible. Jesus will have returned, and all people who have been born since the beginning of time will be raised from the dead (1 Cor. 15:51; 1 Thess. 4:15–17). This means countless billions. After all, "the dead will be raised imperishable, and we shall be changed" (1 Cor. 15:52). The resurrection of Jesus ensures that all—saved and lost—will be raised (v. 22). Even the sea gave up the dead (Rev. 20:13). Some will enjoy eternal bliss in the presence of God, but others will suffer conscious eternal punishment (Matt. 25:46).

The Gospel Will Be Vindicated

The judgment seat of Christ will demonstrate that Jesus the God-man is the only way to the Father (John 14:6) and the only way to be saved (Acts 4:12). It will show that the crucifixion of Jesus appeased the wrath of God and that the resurrection of Jesus took Satan by complete surprise (1 Cor. 2:8). It will clearly demonstrate that we are justified by faith and that being born again is a work of the Holy Spirit and a prerequisite to entering the kingdom of God. In a few words: The judgment seat of Christ will vindicate sound theology.

God Will Clear His Name

Whereas the very presence of the judgment seat of Christ will instantly vindicate the Bible, this in itself would not answer the question of the problem of evil. As I said earlier, if there was no problem of evil there would be no need for faith. God has decreed that *faith* is the means by which he will be affirmed and worshipped. But that does not explain why countless people have suffered over the ages. I have no idea of precisely when God will clear his name during the time of the final judgment. But God promised to do this. We will have to wait until that moment—it is a moment that all of us are looking forward to.

Every Knee Will Bow to the Lord Jesus Christ

This is what Paul said twice, in Romans 14:11 and in Philippians 2:9–11. This does not mean that everyone will be saved—far from it. It means that every single human being will acknowledge who Jesus is and will be forced to get on his or her knees to confess that Jesus of Nazareth is God the Son and the Son of God. All religions of the earth will at last be in total agreement. Every Hindu, every Muslim, every Confucian, and all who adhere to any one but the name above all names will acknowledge the true God.

Justice at Every Level Will Be Administered

The same God who promised that "every valley shall be lifted up, and every mountain and hill be made low" (Isa. 40:4) will demonstrate how the humble will be exalted and the proud will be shattered. Every human being ever born—rich, poor, crippled, blind, brilliant, simple, neglected, and famous—will get full and equal attention from God. This is when the activities and motives of all people that were "hidden in darkness" (1 Cor. 4:5) will be out in the open. This is when the faithful will be rewarded and the hypocrites exposed. We sometimes hear of war veterans who get some kind of recognition belatedly—like in their old age. But the judgment seat of Christ will take note of the weakest and least-known saint from the beginning!

GROUPS OR INDIVIDUALS?

Will God call groups together to witness how a person was maligned? If you have been deeply hurt, wrongly treated, and were emotionally damaged, how will God reveal what happened? And before whom? Will he call the people who know about this to witness his verdict? Will he bring in a video replay to show what was said about you, who said it, when and where it was said, and how you reacted? Are you happy for this to take place? Are you sure that you are on the side of truth? What if God brings the video replay for you to see before your enemy? Does the person who caused the problem have no merit in what he or she has said? What if this person is vindicated rather than you?

God will vindicate the truth—not necessarily individuals.

Let us take the Apostle Paul, for example. He was accused of being unfaithful to the Mosaic law by those who knew little or nothing about the law. The Judaizers, as they are now known, turned some of Paul's own converts against him! Christians in Galatia and Corinth said (in so many words), "Paul, you have let us down by not telling us about the law." That must have been very hard for him to take! I have even wondered if his thorn in the flesh was the Judaizers and if his greatest trial described in 2 Corinthians 1 was caused by the Judaizers. In any case, Paul said that it was "a very small thing" (1 Cor. 4:3–4) to be judged by his opponents and that God would one day reveal the truth. How this will happen can only lead us to what I trust is benign, sanctified speculation. I am sure that God has a better idea than a video replay. But, somehow, the truth will be out and all will be there to see it. I myself am eager to see it!

I look forward to lots of moments at the final judgment (forgive me). I wonder how it will be done. Will I be as exonerated as I think? Could it be my day of great embarrassment? In the meantime, I must "not pronounce judgment before the time" (4:5). The Supreme God of heaven and earth will provide a way of showing the full truth at every level on every issue.

BROADER ISSUES

RACISM

This knotty, painful problem is not limited to the United States. It exists everywhere and at all times. Whereas we in America are conscious of the way African Americans are treated, this matter is a red-hot issue with Indians and Pakistanis; with Koreans and Japanese; and with the French and the English—where the color of one's skin is not what one thinks about. The Apostle Paul even agreed with the statement "Cretans are always liars" (Titus 1:12). Will this sort of thing come up at the judgment? Certainly. Cretans may ask what God thinks. *Everything will come out at God's judgment.* He is a God of glory and a God of justice. This will be his moment to show justice to all his creation—saved and lost.

As for African Americans, they have suffered at the hands of white people—including Christians—more than many of us want to think about. Rude jokes by Christians, heartless treatment by Christians, and unspoken hatred toward black people by both Christians and non-Christians will come to light at the judgment seat of Christ. God is angry—very angry indeed—with many of us white Christians for the way we have neglected, rejected, mistreated, and avoided African Americans. Unfortunately, this treatment does not bother many of us in the slightest. But God is bothered. Fellow white Christian, let me ask you: how would you like all your words about black people or to black people to be flashed on a giant screen for all to observe? How would you like to see videos of how black people have been hurt—whether as slaves in the Deep South in the nineteenth century or when they were put at the back of queues in New York in the twenty-first century? There would possibly have been no organization such as Black Lives Matter if white Christians had loved black people as they should. Black lives certainly matter to Jesus. My fear is that many of us don't even want to think about this. But judgment day is coming. We will see everything.

WEALTHY CHRISTIANS AND THE POOR

James deals with this: wealthy Christians held back paying poor Christians who needed income daily. These poor Christians had no defense. Nobody listened to them—they were at the mercy of ruthless, powerful people. All they could do was to cry out to God. James assures these people that "the cries of the harvesters have reached the ears of the Lord of hosts" (James 5:4). I have no idea what happened later. But this is an example of how the underdogs—who are still born-again people in the church—have had extremely difficult relationships with fellow Christians. The judgment seat of Christ will somehow deal with this sort of thing.

WICKEDNESS IN THE WORLD

I mentioned earlier that a theme running through the Bible is that God is for the underdog. But one might not believe this. That is, until he or she comes before the judgment seat of Christ. Whether it is the mafia in New York and Chicago; Nazism in Germany and other parts of the world; sinister cruelty and torture of Christians by Muslims in Ethiopia, Sudan, and Nigeria; persecution by Hindus in India; those being sexually abused by church leaders; unfair trials all over the world where people get away with murder, judges are paid off, and vindication is withheld from the innocent; people being sentenced to prison unfairly; lies that ruin a person's reputation for life; poor people without insurance being turned away at hospitals; politicians who manage to steal elections; or ruthless people who rape children or sell them into slavery for financial profit, God will have a way with dealing with *every case* at the judgment seat of Christ. People who managed to escape trial for their crimes will not have any place to run when Jesus sets up the great white throne. They may try hiding in the mountains, and famous people will cry to the rocks, "Fall on us and hide us from the face of him who is seated on the throne" (Rev. 6:16), but the angels of God will find them and escort them to the highest court in the universe. No one will resist this summons.

GOLD, SILVER, PRECIOUS STONES, WOOD, HAY, STRAW

Paul uses building material metaphors to depict the choices a Christian makes in following Jesus after he or she has been born again—gold, silver, precious stones, wood, hay, and straw. The foundation of this superstructure is Jesus Christ (1 Cor. 3:11). As born-again believers we are birthed on the solid foundation of Jesus. This assures us that we will go to heaven and not to hell. But we are still required to build a superstructure. The materials we can choose to build it with include gold, silver, precious stones, wood, hay, or straw. The appearance may look fine to everybody; after all, man looks on the appearance. However, God looks on the heart (1 Sam. 16:7). The ingredients we use to build the super-structure will be displayed and tested at the judgment seat of Christ. Here are Paul's words on this:

> Each one's work will become manifest, for the Day will dis-close it, because it will be revealed by fire, and the fire will test what sort of work each one has done. If the work that anyone has built on the foundation survives, he will receive a reward. If anyone's work is burned up, he will suffer loss, though he himself will be saved, but only as through fire. (1 Cor. 3:13–15)

These verses show that there are not only rewards at the judg-ment seat of Christ, but that a person can lose his or her reward and still be eternally saved. I don't know how this will happen, but all Christians will go through "fire" on that day. If our super-structure is built with the imperishable materials that will survive fire—gold, silver, and precious stones—a reward follows. If one has built a superstructure with materials that may be consumed by fire such as wood, hay, and straw, there will be nothing left. This is what Paul means by saying that one will lose his or her reward yet will be saved, "but only as through fire."

Comparably, in 1 Corinthians 9 Paul uses the words "prize" and "wreath" ("crown," KJV) as synonyms of "reward" (9:24–25).

A reward was very important to Paul—important enough for him to say, "I discipline my body and keep it under control, lest after preaching to others I myself should be disqualified" (v. 27). That is, he would be disqualified for the prize or reward. Here is another translation: "I strike a blow to my body and make it my slave so that after I have preached to others, I myself will not be disqualified for the prize" (NIV). It is interesting that when Paul wrote these words, probably between AD 50 and AD 55, he himself was not sure that he would get a reward. But in AD 65, when Paul was waiting to be beheaded at any moment, he declared triumphantly:

> The time of my departure has come. I have fought the good fight, I have finished the race, I have kept the faith. Henceforth there is laid up for me the crown of righteousness, which the Lord, the righteous judge, will award to me on that day, and not only to me but also to all who have loved his appearing. (2 Tim. 4:6–8)

How do we know whether we are building a superstructure with gold, silver, precious stones?

Seek to do things that please God. If you and I live lives focused on pleasing God, I can safely say that we are building our superstructure with the right materials! Fire will not burn these up.

COMING INTO YOUR INHERITANCE

Those who come into their inheritance will receive a reward. Some obtain their inheritance, but some don't. If you do, you will be given a crown of righteousness at the judgment seat of Christ. To those who forgive, rid themselves of bitterness, resist sexual temptation, dignify trials, and walk in the light God gives us, two things follow: you are coming into your inheritance, and you will be awarded a prize at the judgment seat of Christ.

YOU WILL BE JUDGED BY WHAT YOU ARE AS A PERSON, NOT YOUR SUCCESS IN LIFE

If I should be given a reward at the judgment seat of Christ, it will not be based upon any success in my ministry. If you add together how many times I have preached, how many sermons I have prepared, how many books I have written, and how many people were converted to Christ under my ministry, I can tell you these things will have *nothing to do* with my receiving a reward.

Any reward given to me will be based on what kind of husband and father I have been, and on what kind of personal character I have had. The same is true with you, reader. It will not be your job, your education, your promotions, your reputation, or your money earned that will contribute to your reward. It will be whether you walk in the light, have embraced sexual purity in your personal life, and have lived a life of total forgiveness.

Whereas the aforementioned things will survive the fire of judgment, displeasing God ends badly, as I mentioned earlier in this book. Displeasing God is the way to build a superstructure of wood, hay, and straw. Guaranteed. This means choosing to forfeit your inheritance. I feel so sorry when I see this happen. This makes me very sad.

The purpose of the teaching of the judgment seat of Christ is to change lives. We do not merely anticipate this coming event; it should have an impact on our lives right now. In other words, when we know that everything hidden will be revealed in the day of judgment, we need to fall upon our knees to reevaluate what we have said and believed. And, if truth calls for it, we must seek to put things right while there is still time. Speaking for myself, the teaching of the judgment seat of Christ has had more influence on my personal and private life than any other part of my theology.

Some Concluding Thoughts on the Judgment Seat of Christ, Especially for the Convicted Soul

We all have many questions regarding the nature of a reward at the judgment. We cannot help but be curious. What will a reward from Jesus be like? A literal crown? A huge mansion? A star in one's crown?

I close this section with the surest and most comforting thought I know. God is the God of the "second look," as John Newton put it in his hymn, "In Evil Long I Took Delight":

> A second look He gave, which said,
> "I freely all forgive;
> This blood is for thy ransom paid;
> I die that thou mayest live."

God came to Jonah a "second time" (Jonah 3:1). He is the God of the "second chance" (and also the third, and the fourth . . .). Yes. What a God!

You might be wondering why I have written so much about judgment. Are you convinced that you have totally forfeited your inheritance? Is there no hope? On the contrary, there is hope. As surely as God lives and as surely as the Holy Spirit convicts you, there is hope. He would not convict you and woo you if there were no hope. He is on your case.

If the truth be told, there is hardly a single Christian on the planet who has not worried about some fault, some mistake, some sin, some unguarded comment, or some egregious act. It is a safe bet to assume that he or she feels horrible and therefore suffers from guilt. Just for your information, I head the list. I can categorically testify: God is gracious. His mercy endures forever. He is no respecter of persons.

If you struggled through what I have written in this section and have never prayed to God for forgiveness, I want to reassure you that there is hope. I suggest you pray this prayer now.

Lord Jesus, I have failed you. I am so sorry. Have mercy on me. Thank you for dying on the cross for me. Graciously forgive me of all my sin and failure. I rededicate my life wholly and entirely to you. Thank you for your mercy. Amen.

May the blessing of God the Father, God the Son, and God the Holy Spirit, together with the sprinkling of the blood of Jesus, be yours now and evermore. Amen.

Thus far we have looked at what pleases God and why we should seek to please God. In the next section, I will talk about how we should please God.

PART III

HOW SHOULD WE
PLEASE GOD?

CHAPTER 7

FINDING OUT WHAT MATTERS MOST TO GOD

❧

For thou hast magnified thy word above all
thy name.
—PSALM 138:2 KJV

It doesn't matter how rich, talented, cool, or attractive you
are; integrity matters most.
—ANONYMOUS

What matters most to you? Can you honestly put your finger on the number one item that gives you more satisfaction and pleasure than anything else? If someone wanted to please you—and hoped to please you to the hilt—could you tell them what that item is?

Some years ago a friend wanted to take me to my absolute favorite restaurant in London for my birthday.

"Are you sure?" I asked him.

"Yes," he replied.

"OK, take me to Fakhreldine's in Piccadilly." This was a famous Arab restaurant, known for its falafels, hummus, kebabs, and garlic tomatoes.

He was quiet for a moment, then replied, "I have a better idea."

"OK, where?" I asked.

He wanted to take me to a less expensive restaurant around the corner from my choice.

"But you said you wanted to take me to my favorite restaurant," I responded.

"But you will like this one better," he shot back.

"No," I retorted. "You have picked a cheaper restaurant. You have chosen a restaurant that pleases *you* the most, not the one that pleases *me* the most."

What do you suppose pleases God the most? Is there a way to find out? Remember that it is not what pleases *you* the most *about* God, but what actually pleases *him* the most—in himself. Would he have a first choice? Would he tell us if he did?

As far as I am able to tell, Psalm 138:2 ("thou hast magnified thy word above all thy name" [KJV]) comes the closest to finding out what means the most to God. You might say this: surely it would be his glory and honor. Agreed. And that is precisely what Psalm 138:2 is telling us. Now bear with me.

First, there are two ways by which God reveals himself in the Bible: *his name and his word.* Let's begin with his name. How important do you suppose God's name is to him? I can tell you: a lot. He is, after all, a God of glory—a jealous God. You could easily make a case that the most important thing of all to God Almighty is his name. Consider Exodus 6:2–3:

I am the Lord. I appeared to Abraham, to Isaac, and to Jacob, as
God Almighty, but by my name the Lord I did not make myself
known to them.

With the unveiling of God's name came unprecedented signs
and wonders and miracles: the burning bush, the ten plagues on
Egypt, the crossing of the Red Sea on dry land, the manna, and
other awesome displays of God's presence in the wilderness. You
don't find such phenomena with Abraham, Isaac, or Jacob. So,
based on Exodus 6:3, one might easily conclude that the name of
the Lord would mean most to God Almighty. The name shows
God's power and reputation, which spread all over that part of
the world due to the signs and wonders. Moses wanted to protect
and preserve God's reputation. For instance, when God himself
said that he would destroy Israel and start with Moses all over
again (Num. 14:12), Moses urged God to change his mind, saying: "Now if you kill this people as one man, then the nations
who have heard your fame will say, 'It is because the Lord was
not able to bring this people into the land that he swore to give
to them'" (vv. 15–16). Moses knew the esteem God had for his
own name, and God was pleased with him for interceding for the
Israelites. Centuries later when Jesus gave his disciples what is
known as the Lord's Prayer, the very first petition is: "Hallowed
be your name" (Matt. 6:9). So make no mistake: God esteems
his name.

And yet, strange as it may seem, Psalm 138:2 as literally
translated from the Hebrew reads: "You have exalted your word
above all your name." Only the King James Version translates the
Hebrew verbatim. The English Standard Version gives the literal

translation in a footnote. All other versions that I know of avoid this direct translation. Why? I am not sure. Perhaps because it is hard to believe that God would want his word exalted above his name.

But this should not surprise us. Whereas name refers to reputation, word refers to integrity. God cares more about his integrity than he does his reputation. Time is on God's side; he can wait. One day God will make sure that his name is cleared by vindicating his honor and wisdom to the world. Every knee shall bow and every tongue will confess to God's honor and power. To those who say, "God has a lot to answer for" because he has allowed evil to continue when he could have stopped it, I answer: God will have the last word—but he will not clear his name until the last day.

In the meantime, God will allow people to question his name, his wisdom, and what he does and permits. And he will not step in to intervene. But when King David said, "You have magnified your word above all your name," he showed how well he truly knew God. While I do not mean to prove anything, I suggest that David was letting the world see why God called him a man after his own heart. Many, many people over the centuries could have told you a lot about God. But there is a difference between knowing about God and knowing him.

A person can know a lot about the Grand Canyon without going there. A person can be an expert on the American Civil War without traveling to Gettysburg or Atlanta. I became attracted to bonefishing in the Florida Keys and the Bahamas for a long time without success. But one day I finally caught my first bonefish and I was not prepared for the feeling I got from it. Also, I knew a lot about Billy Graham and even spent nearly two hours with him one day. But I cannot honestly say I truly knew Billy Graham—I only found out a bit more about him. I do know my wife Louise. I know my son, T. R. I could name a few people that I truly know. And I would like to say that I know the Lord. Even Paul, who possibly knew Jesus Christ better than anybody, kept this desire burning: to "know him" (Phil. 3:10).

King David knew the Lord. He knew what matters most to God. Therefore, when it came to God's word, David knew that God's honor and integrity were on the line. *That is what matters most to God.* Furthermore, this is why the New Testament *twice* states that it is impossible for God to lie (Titus 1:2; Heb. 6:18). The God of the Bible is a God of *truth*: "Once for all I have sworn by my holiness; I will not lie to David" (Ps. 89:35). When we get to heaven, I would not be surprised to learn that David knew the Lord more intimately than anyone in the Old Testament other than Moses and Abraham. Here is one example of Moses's intimate knowledge of God:

> The Rock, his work is perfect,
>> for all his ways are justice.
> A God of faithfulness and without iniquity,
>> just and upright is he. (Deut. 32:4)

And here is what God's one and only Son said:

> I am the way, and the *truth*, and the life. (John 14:6, emphasis mine)

Do you want to please God? Honor his word. Believe in his word. Trust in his word. Be willing to die for his word. So I ask again: Do you want to know what matters most to God and his relationship to you, dear reader? That you believe his word. Do you want to know what gives God the greatest pleasure? When his children trust in his word.

The first step to pleasing God, then, is to honor his word. The Bible is God's integrity put on the line.

Satan works overtime day and night to get people to doubt God's word. He gets into Bible colleges and seminaries to get students to doubt God's word. The first thing the serpent did with Eve in the garden of Eden was to get her to doubt God's word: "Did God actually say, 'You shall not eat of any tree in the garden'?" (Gen. 3:1). The first thing Satan tried to do with Jesus when tempting him in the wilderness by saying "If you are the Son of God . . ." (Matt. 4:3) was to have him doubt God.

Moses was forbidden to enter the promised land because he did not believe God's word in a crucial moment. The children of Israel died in the wilderness within forty years because they did not believe God's word to follow Joshua and Caleb and conquer Canaan at the beginning of the forty years.

In a sentence: God can wait for universal vindication. He will have his day—one day.

But God has now put his integrity on the line—his word. Integrity matters most to God. It should also matter most to you and me.

If you want to find a fast track on how to please God, start with trusting his word.

Someone asked me three or four years ago, "What would you like to accomplish most in your lifetime?" My answer now is the same as then: to get people to believe the Bible.

WE ARE SAVED BY GOD'S WORD

You will recall that God did not reveal his name to Abraham, Isaac, and Jacob. The spectacular miracles came simultaneously with God revealing his name to Moses. The patriarchs followed God and heard God—by his word. There were neither signs nor miracles to confirm the word; only their faith propelled them to keep going.

One night God said to Abraham, "Look toward heaven, and number the stars," adding, "So shall your offspring be" (Gen. 15:5). At that time Sarah—aged about 75—was barren. Abraham was an old man—aged 85. Why should Abraham ever believe such a word? He might easily have replied, "You must be joking. Do you expect me to believe that?"

But Abraham believed this word! What is more, God counted Abraham's faith as "righteousness" (v. 6). That moment became the Apostle Paul's Exhibit A for his teaching of justification by faith alone.

Why is this important? We are saved by hearing and believing God's word—not by seeing miracles. The era of the patriarchs was characterized by hearing and believing the word of the Lord. They had sheer faith in the word. This is a sobering reminder that the gospel of Jesus Christ is based upon faith in God's word. It pleases God through the folly of what is preached to save those who believe (1 Cor. 1:21). It is the message contained in Paul's letter to the Romans—what Martin Luther called "the purest gospel"— that saves people. This is what we are to preach.

"The word is near you, in your mouth and in your heart" (that is, the word of faith that we proclaim); because, if you confess

with your mouth that Jesus is Lord and believe in your heart
that God raised him from the dead, you will be saved. . . .
So faith comes from hearing, and hearing through the word of
Christ. (Rom. 10:8–9, 17)

The Apostle Paul believed in miracles. He saw people healed
in his own ministry—he even raised a man from the dead. He
refers to "the power of signs and wonders" in the same book of
Romans (15:19). But Paul seeks to support his teaching of justification by faith alone by going back to Abraham—before the era of
miracles. Paul might have said, "I am not ashamed of the gospel
of the kingdom." He did believe in the kingdom. Paul might have
said, "I am not ashamed of the gospel of healing." He did believe
in healing. But one of Paul's opening statements in Romans—
his longest book and the one that gives the most detail on the
gospel—is this: "I am not ashamed of the gospel, for it is the power
of God for *salvation*" (1:16, emphasis mine).

Salvation is what fits us for heaven. A person could be healed
but still be eternally lost. A person could see others raised from
the dead but miss seeing Jesus. After all, many Jews saw Lazarus
after he was raised from the dead, but some of them still opposed
Jesus (John 11:45–46ff).

WE ARE GUIDED BY
GOD'S WORD

The writer to the Hebrews described the word of God as "living
and active, sharper than any two-edged sword, piercing to the divi-
sion of soul and of spirit, of joints and of marrow, and discerning

the thoughts and intentions of the heart" (Heb. 4:12). One must remember that when the New Testament refers to Scripture, it refers to the Old Testament:

> All Scripture is breathed out by God and profitable for teaching, for reproof, for correction, and for training in righteousness, that the man of God may be complete, equipped for every good work. (2 Tim. 3:16–17)

> No prophecy of Scripture comes from someone's own interpretation. For no prophecy was ever produced by the will of man, but men spoke from God as they were carried along by the Holy Spirit. (2 Pet. 1:20–21)

But when Peter referred to Paul's letters, he elevated them to the level of Holy Scripture:

> Our beloved brother Paul also wrote to you according to the wisdom given him, as he does in all his letters when he speaks in them of these matters. There are some things in them that are hard to understand, which the ignorant and unstable twist to their own destruction, as they do the other Scriptures. (3:15–16)

DOES GOD SPEAK ONLY THROUGH SCRIPTURE?

How else might we understand the meaning of the term "word of God"? Would it include prophetic utterances as described in the

New Testament? Paul does say that we should not "despise prophecies" but test them (1 Thess. 5:20–21). This shows that we are not to regard prophetic words as infallible or receive them uncritically. In my book *Prophetic Integrity* I suggest seven levels of prophecy, the highest being Holy Scripture.

Dr. Martyn Lloyd-Jones used to say again and again that the Bible was not given to replace direct revelation but to correct abuses. He shared personal stories with me about God speaking directly to him. *Any word that conflicts with Holy Scripture is false.* But to say that the Bible is the only way God can speak is to quench the Holy Spirit. Any word from God will affirm and cohere with Holy Scripture.

When we stand our ground against the schemes of the devil, Paul admonishes us to take "the sword of the Spirit, which is the word of God" (Eph. 6:17). Did he mean the Bible? Or was he asking the Ephesians to know the Old Testament? He could not mean the New Testament, which was still being written. And yet the language used in Hebrews 4:12 also describes what comes out of Jesus's mouth: "a sharp two-edged sword" (Rev. 1:16). Chapters two and three of the book of Revelation are seven letters from Jesus seated at the right hand of God. Thus, what Jesus said became part of the canon and was Holy Scripture.

Job said he esteemed the words that came from God's mouth more than his necessary food (Job 23:12). Was he referring to books in the Old Testament? Possibly.

Therefore, even though there is a gray area about what the word of God actually is, God himself knows *when* he has spoken and *whether* we have heard from him. As solid expository preaching imparts the word of God—for which hearers are responsible—so God knows what we have received from him. As I relate in my book *Prophetic Integrity*, when the elderly evangelist Dr. W. M. Tidwell warned the congregation, "Someone here is getting their last call to be saved," it was a no-nonsense, no-joke moment which proved to be the word of God. We cannot play games with God; he knows both what we know and whether we have been recipients of his word, responsible for what we have heard.

I believe that only the Bible—the sixty-six books of Holy Scripture—is infallible. But I would be dishonest and a hypocrite— and only trying to avoid possible criticism—if I denied what I know to be true about God's word not being limited to Scripture. This chapter is, after all, largely about integrity—God's and ours.

I can testify that there have been times when the Spirit of God spoke directly to me. It has not happened often—in fact, less than a dozen instances in my lifetime. But when God spoke, I had no doubt. I once heard a voice telling me to "turn to Philippians 1:12," a verse I did not know. This utterance of God's word changed my life forever. When I heard the words "your ministry in America will be to charismatics" some two years before I retired from Westminster Chapel, my heart sank—but I knew this was from the Lord. I have had visions—not many, but a few—that were unquestionably from the Holy Spirit. I will not enter into the speculative discussion of whether these words were *logos* or *rhema*, both being Greek for "word," but I cherish every instance when God spoke. I would *not* make these words equal to Holy Scripture—but I believe they were true and from God.

As I mentioned earlier, Louise had an accident during our time at Westminster when her ear drum was punctured. She felt strongly that she should learn sign language. But was this leading from the Lord? It was not my idea. One morning, Alex Buchanan, an Englishman from Yorkshire who was known as a prophet, phoned me. He asked to speak to Louise, and said to her, "God is leading you to do something that is not your husband's idea but yours, and you should pursue this." She subsequently learned sign language. By the time we retired from Westminster Chapel, we had between twenty and thirty deaf people attending regularly. Several of them became Christians.

When Jesus addressed the church of Ephesus from the right hand of God, he complimented them for several things. But he still lamented, "You have abandoned the love you had at first" (Rev. 2:4). That first love was the gospel. Paul had earlier warned that there would be a falling away (2 Thess. 2:1ff), and the book of Revelation was written during the final decade of the first century AD. This was the beginning of the era of the apostolic fathers. Scholarly studies have been done on the doctrines of grace in the writings of the apostolic fathers, concluding that there was hardly any preaching on grace during that time. Christianity had become almost sheer morality. Strange as it may seem, it is difficult to find a clear teaching of the gospel until you get to St. Augustine centuries later.

Pleasing God truly begins when we make his word our priority—that we believe it, trust in it, and are not ashamed of it. The word that motivated the patriarchs is what gave rise to the gospel. We begin to please God by loving his word.

CHAPTER 8

LIVING OUTSIDE OF
YOUR COMFORT ZONE

❦

For the desires of the flesh are against the Spirit, and the
desires of the Spirit are against the flesh, for these are
opposed to each other, to keep you from doing the things you
want to do.

—GALATIANS 5:17

Science, they say, can tap the brain of man and alter his
desires. But the Bible, which has withstood the ravages of
time . . . says that we are possessed of a sinful, fallen nature
which wars against us.

—BILLY GRAHAM (1918–2018)

Pleasing God is an act of the will. Although it arises from a desire put in one's heart by the Holy Spirit, pleasing God follows an act of the will. It will frequently mean going outside your comfort zone. It also means overriding what is not naturally easy. Although

God implants this desire in us, don't expect him to knock you down to make it happen! You must decide, and you must act. If pleasing God came naturally, then all people would inevitably please God.

I could wish that saving faith—being born again—would eradicate the sinful nature. I could also wish that a second work of grace, as I was taught while growing up, would enable a person to live above sin. Even though I went to the altar time and time again to get sanctified wholly, I never arrived at the goal I hoped I would reach. I will admit that I had an amazing victory after my previously mentioned experience of October 31, 1955. For a few months I enjoyed enormous peace and ability to resist temptations of many kinds. But one day this ended. We must come to terms with this truth: we won't be free from the presence of sin until we get to heaven and are "glorified" (Rom. 8:30)—that is, "changed" (1 Cor. 15:51).

When Paul said that the flesh wars against the Spirit and the Spirit against the flesh, he was referring to all Christians generally and himself particularly. As I noted earlier, "If we *say* we have no sin, we deceive ourselves, and the truth is not in us" (1 John 1:8, emphasis mine). John was speaking from experience. Paul was also speaking from experience. And Jeremiah was speaking from experience when he said that "the heart is deceitful above all things" and incurably wicked (Jer. 17:9). Enoch was born in sin like all of us, but he had the witness that he pleased God and left a legacy that would inspire us to please God.

So how do we please God? By overcoming the initial dislike, threat, or challenge we are faced with. This is not merely resisting our dislike; this is overcoming it and getting an internal victory over it. It is about what happens in the heart. And, yes, this will almost certainly mean going outside your comfort zone.

SEXUAL TEMPTATION

We naturally dislike the Bible's prohibition against sex outside of marriage since God made us with sexual desire, which is a physical urge. In the garden of Eden God made humankind "male and female" (Gen. 1:27) in order to populate the earth. We are also born with these two basic needs: (1) the desire for sexual gratification and (2) the need for significance. It is hard to say which of these two is the stronger. However, sexual gratification is not essential for living, as opposed to the need for food—which we must meet in order to live.

I was very close to Dr. Martyn Lloyd-Jones—we were like father and son. One day I told him that I continued to struggle with sexual temptation, both before and after my marriage. He surprised me by saying, "All my life I have had the same struggle," which reassured me (by knowing that even the great Doctor was like the rest of us). Indeed, virtually all preachers struggle with sexual temptation. Sadly, too many have had to leave the ministry because of failure in this area. When I hear of a preacher falling, I say to myself, "That's me but by the grace of God."

Because sexual desire is a natural, physical urge, many reckon they have a right to indulge in this area as they please. But the same God who made us this way also laid down permanent perimeters in this area. For instance, sexual intercourse must only happen in a heterosexual marriage. Premarital sex and sex outside marriage is sin. This is enforced by the Ten Commandments and outlined in many Mosaic commands in Leviticus and Deuteronomy. The same standard is clear throughout the New Testament. Likewise, homosexual practice was equally forbidden.

In a few words: We all must resist what God has forbidden,

however great the temptation may be. This pleases God. For example, Joseph could not have known he was earmarked to be the future prime minister of Egypt when he resisted sexual temptation by Potiphar's wife (Gen. 39). How many good people have blown away a brilliant future because they gave in to this kind of sin? The man I was named after, Dr. R. T. Williams, would counsel young preachers: "Beware of two things in your ministry: money and women. For if a scandal regarding either of these should break out, God will forgive you but the people won't." The world *loves* to hear news about a high-profile Christian falling into sexual sin. Do not give the devil that pleasure!

The Family

After God declared that humankind is "male and female," he introduced marriage and children. The family idea was thus born in the garden of Eden. Here I refer to husband, wife, and children—this group is sometimes called the "nuclear family." As Sir Thomas Browne (1605–1682) said, "Charity begins at home." This is a good statement but challenging. If you are going to demonstrate love but practice it with everyone but your own family, you are possibly not only sweeping the dirt under the carpet but also running from the greatest challenge anyone ever has faced. It can be a lot easier to show love and kindness with people you hardly know than at home. When I give a sermon after marrying a couple, I often quote Paul's words: "Husbands, love your wives" (Eph. 5:25). No couple thinks they need to hear this on their honeymoon! But my caution is this: the honeymoon will end. Paul's word for "love" in Ephesians 5:25 is from the Greek *agape*—not *eros*. *Agape* is unselfish love; *eros* is physical love. Martin Luther once said that God uses sex to drive a man to marriage, ambition to drive him to service, and fear to drive him to faith. But the *eros* love that may motivate a person to get married is not the love that will sustain it. At some stage, usually soon after the honeymoon, *agape* must not replace but come alongside *eros*.

Louise and I have been married for almost sixty-five years. I can undoubtedly testify that I cannot even come close to a sense of pleasing God when I fail to make my wife feel loved. I then cannot enjoy friends, tasting the best food, preaching to the world, or preparing sermons. And pleasing my wife is not always easy. However, it is perhaps even harder for the wife to submit to her husband. I must not wait for my wife to submit before I love her, and she must not delay submitting until she feels loved. We each have a duty before God: I must love her whether or not she submits; she must love me whether or not she feels loved.

Although this task of loving our spouse can be very hard, we must begin here if we truly want to please God. This can be the hardest thing on earth to do—I am sure of it. But it is a crucial litmus test as to whether we want to please God. If I say, "I am going to please God, but I refuse to love my wife," I am walking in black darkness. Loving one's wife may not be easy, and *God knows* whether a husband is doing this. Likewise, submitting to a harsh, unreasonable husband may not be easy—divorce may be the only way out—but *God knows* whether a wife is doing her best.

The greatest sense of guilt I have ever felt in my lifetime has been over my neglect of my family while my children were growing up. At Oxford I put my studies first, and at Westminster Chapel I put my church and sermon preparation first—thinking

I was putting God first. I now believe that had I put my family first, I would have preached just as well—but I cannot get those years back.

The Enemy

Jesus assumed that all of us would have enemies. Otherwise, why would he say, "Love your enemies" (Matt. 5:44)? Or why would he include the petition in the Lord's Prayer, "Forgive us our sins, for we ourselves forgive everyone who is indebted to us" (Luke 11:4)?

We all have a story to tell. We all feel that the injustice we receive in our particular case is so horrible that God would not expect us to forgive such a deed. We all honestly believe that we are the exception to the rule. I am sorry, but the truth is that there are no exceptions to the rule. Nevertheless, the more important truth is this: the greater the hurt—or injustice—perpetrated against us, the greater the blessing of God will be to us—if we forgive. The greater the suffering is, the greater the anointing will be. I can honestly say that the greatest hurt of my whole life is the greatest thing that has ever happened to me! It can be that way with you too—I promise.

You may recall that I said in chapter 1 that your wife can be your enemy. For instance, John Wesley (1703–1791) had an unhappy marriage. His wife would even make insulting gestures and mocking noises during his preaching! I have often wondered if Wesley's teaching on perfect love came out of his own experience at home. George Whitefield (1714–1770) also had troubles in his marriage. He was jilted by the girl he truly loved, then married someone he loved less. However, thousands of sovereign vessels in heaven will report that their difficult marriage was part of the key to their being used of God.

> God moves in a mysterious way,
> His wonders to perform;
> He plants his footsteps in the sea,
> And rides upon the storm.
>
> —WILLIAM COWPER (1731–1800)

The devil does not want you to forgive (2 Cor. 2:10–11); he wants an entry into your life. Thus, when you hold a grudge and will not forgive totally, he will mess up your mind, your judgment, and even your happiness. His greatest ally is your anger and unforgiveness; don't give him that pleasure! Besides, if you want to please God you will have to get to this place sooner or later.

I cannot go into such detail as my book *Total Forgiveness* did, but I urge you to be sure of these seven things:

1. TELL NO ONE WHAT HE OR SHE DID TO YOU—TELL GOD. Our first temptation when we have been hurt is to tell people what "they" did. When you totally forgive, step number one is to refuse to tell anyone what he or she did. There are two exceptions: first, tell one person for therapeutic reasons—someone who will tell nobody. Second, a crime must be reported.

2. DON'T LET PEOPLE BE AFRAID OF YOU OR NERVOUS AROUND YOU. Put them at ease; one day they will praise

you for this. "Perfect love casts out fear" (1 John 4:18). Total forgiveness will refuse to make others feel afraid.

3. DON'T LET PEOPLE FEEL GUILTY—NEVER THROW UP WHAT THEY DID. Don't rub their noses in it. When God forgives us he does not throw up our past to us, because he wants us to forgive ourselves.

4. LET OTHERS SAVE FACE. In his book *How to Win Friends and Influence People*, Dale Carnegie reckons that if you let others save face, you win friends for life. This means not only to behave as though they did nothing wrong, but also to cover for them so that they retain their dignity.

5. PROTECT PEOPLE FROM FEARING YOU WILL REVEAL THEIR DARK SECRETS. Assure people that no one will ever know what you know about them.

6. PRAY FOR OTHERS—AND SINCERELY MEAN IT—FOR GOD TO BLESS THEM. This is probably the greatest test of all. But when you do this—and really, really mean it— you're probably *there*. Don't tell them you are praying for them; this would be counterproductive. This type of prayer is your secret to a greater anointing of the Holy Spirit.

7. COMMIT TO PRACTICING TOTAL FORGIVENESS FOR THE REST OF YOUR LIFE. Total forgiveness is a life sentence. Like a tablet the doctor gives you which you will need for the rest of your life, total forgiveness is something you keep doing until the day you die.

Putting these seven principles into practice will lead you to the high road of pleasing God. You might call it "the road less traveled":

Two roads diverged in a wood, and I,
I took the one less traveled by,
And that has made all the difference.

—ROBERT FROST (1874–1963)

A greater blessing and usefulness is on the way.

THE TRIAL

As Jesus said, "In the world you will have tribulation" (John 16:33). He did not come to this earth to eliminate fiery trials but to get into the fire with us. James began his short letter with an extraordinary challenge, "Count it all joy"—the NIV says "pure joy"—when we face trials of various kinds (James 1:2). However, as the most natural feeling in the world is to want vengeance when we are mistreated, so also our natural impulse is to grumble when a sudden trial comes upon us. Nevertheless, as James said, we actually need to count it joy if we "fall"—*peripto* in Greek—into a trial. This is important because one might say that if trials bring joy, I should go out looking for a trial. No—don't do that! The trial will come soon enough. That said, there is a condition for counting it joy in a trial: if you *fall* into it. That means you did not make the trial happen. You did not cause it; it happened to you. That means you may take this trial as coming from God. See these lines from the hymn "Like a River Glorious":

Every joy or trial
Falleth from above,
Traced upon our dial

> By the Sun of Love;
> We may trust Him fully
> All for us to do.
> They who trust Him wholly
> Find Him wholly true.
>
> —FRANCES RIDLEY HAVERGAL (1836–1879)

This is why Jesus told us to pray, "Lead us not *into* temptation" (Matt. 6:13, emphasis mine). The word "temptation" comes from *peirismos*, meaning "testing," "trial," or "temptation." In other words, although Jesus told us that in this world we are going to have trials, we should still pray not to have them! We should pray daily that God will be pleased *not to let us face testing*. Don't ask for it; pray against it. But . . . if it comes, then take it with both hands, since God has allowed it for a purpose.

That said, when a trial lands upon us, we must make a choice— which will probably mean going outside our comfort zone again. Instead of complaining or feeling sorry for ourselves, we need to try *dignifying the trial*—imputing dignity and honor to it. James's word "count" is the same that Paul uses for "impute," "esteem," or "reckon"; faith is counted, or reckoned, as righteousness (Rom. 4:5). In the same way, we should esteem a trial as joy, not as something bad. Why? First, if God sent this trial, it has to be a good thing. Second, it is only a matter of time before you will look back on this trial and see that it was for your good! So, if you are going to end up esteeming your current trial as a good thing, do it now!

Dignifying the trial means that we should do these five things:

1. ACCEPT THE TRIAL AS FROM GOD. This is the first step. You may not feel like it, but I urge you to pray: "Lord, I

believe this is from you. I don't know why you have let this happen. But this is my chance to show you that I want to please you."

2. DON'T COMPLAIN. We almost automatically tend to start grumbling, "Why can this happen to me? This is not fair." This trial could cost you time. It could cost you money. It will be an inconvenience. Your life—at least for a moment—has changed without your causing it.

3. DON'T TRY TO END THE TRIAL. Let God finish things. This can be the greatest challenge for you to accept—but all trials have a built-in time frame. God is the author of the trial; he started it and will end it. *The trial will end.* We think at first that it never will. But it will. It could end suddenly. At that time, you will know whether you passed the test (by dignifying the trial) or failed it (by complaining so much).

4. LOOK FORWARD TO THE JOY AND SATISFACTION YOU WILL FEEL WHEN THE TRIAL ENDS. Keep determining to dignify the trial. You will never be sorry.

5. LEARN THE PURPOSE GOD HAS FOR YOU IN THIS TIME OF TESTING. Maybe the trial is meant only to teach you patience! As James says, let patience have its "perfect work" (KJV) or "full effect" (James 1:4). In other words, get the complete benefit of it. Some years ago in one of the greatest trials of my life—when a good friend betrayed me—my reading that day was the following passage; I have never forgotten it:

> We rejoice in our sufferings, knowing that suffering produces endurance, and endurance produces character. (Rom. 5:3–4)

I have been the greatest complainer of anybody I know. But one day I decided to preach through James. I knew that "count it all joy when ye fall into divers temptations" (James 1:2 KJV) came at the beginning of the book. Studying and preaching this verse forced me to practice dignifying the trial. This changed my life. Shortly after I preached from James 1:2, a major, major trial landed upon me and Louise. I received a phone call from Scotland Yard, warning me not to drive—not even an inch—because my American driver's license was not valid. I thought it was—but I was wrong. As I put down the phone—it was 3:00 p.m.—Louise walked into the room. I remember our conversation as though it were yesterday.

"I'm going to get the children at school," she said.

"Honey, sit down," I urged.

"Tell me when I get back in a few minutes—I have to go," she replied.

"Honey, please sit down."

"I'm late—and I'm coming right back," she pleaded.

"Louise—either what I preach is true, or it isn't," I insisted.

"Whatever are you talking about?" she queried.

I tried to explain. "We cannot drive the car. Not at all. I have just been told by the police that our driving licenses are not valid. I have been preaching on 'dignifying the trial.' Now we have been given a dandy. We may never have a trial like this again. I am determined to dignify this trial."

We then phoned a friend, who kindly picked up our kids. As it turned out, we could not drive for several months. We had to walk, get a ride from someone, or go on the tube (i.e., subway). Although I had been driving for over twenty-five years, we had to take new driving lessons in order to get a British driver's license.

It is literally easier to get a pilot's license in America than a driver's license in England. An American friend living in England, who had a pilot's license to fly his private plane in the USA, told me this—and he wasn't joking.

Those were difficult days. But they were used of the Lord to enable me to grow spiritually like I had never known before in my life.

When my mother was around twelve years old, she met with a group of children who would periodically sit at the feet of a ninety-year old Christian woman in Springfield, Illinois. The saintly lady said this one day: "I have been serving the Lord for so long now that I can hardly tell the difference between a blessing and a trial."

May these words grip you as they did those youngsters many years ago.

MONEY

Paul warns that "those who desire to be rich fall into temptation, into a snare" (1 Tim. 6:9). This unfortunately does happen to Christians. Greed can be subtle and seemingly innocent. A possessive love of money and what it will buy sneaks into the back door of our lives. We forget that *this world is not all there is*, forgetting that life at its longest is still short. *Just enough* is what God has promised (Matt. 6:33; Phil. 4:19). But just enough is not good enough for many. The love of money—not money but the *love* of it—is a "root of all kinds of evils" (1 Tim. 6:10). It lures many from the faith.

I was born into what could be characterized as lower middle class. My father worked for wages as a rate clerk with the

Chesapeake and Ohio Railway. I can recall him explaining many times how he could not afford the nice things which many others around us had. As I grew up, his salary was $40.00 a week. But he was a faithful tither—$4.00 a week went regularly to our Nazarene church. This was valuable training for life. That said, I don't think I learned then how to handle money. Years later, when I had my major theological shift and was forced to get a job to live, I went into debt. Before I knew it, I owed thousands of dollars and had to postpone full-time ministry for nearly seven years until I was completely out of debt. The silver lining in all my financial folly was that I truly learned to handle money. I also began serious tithing, and have owed no one anything for over sixty years. I have learned that just enough is indeed good enough. But I fear that many never learn this. Dear reader, if you will bear with me, I want to both warn and encourage you to practice two principles (however difficult): (1) live within your income and (2) be a faithful tither. Give God one-tenth of your income regularly. I will say more on this in the next section.

GIVING, ESPECIALLY TO THE NEEDY

Why is it *so* easy to neglect the poor? I have personal experience here. I will almost never feel "led" to reach out to someone who is poor. I used to say to myself, especially when seeing a beggar, "Why doesn't he get a job? There are jobs out there." Yet Jesus said, "You always have the poor with you" (Matt. 26:11). He was not justifying the situation, but reminding us to be conscious that the poor will always be around. Moses gave a similar reminder: "For there will never cease to be poor in the land" (Deut. 15:11). He also sternly warned wealthy people to pay poor people their wages on the same day lest the poor cry against them to the Lord of hosts and they be guilty of sin (24:15).

Many biblical statements, as we will see next, clearly hint that there will always be at least one quick way to please God—namely, reach out to the poor.

> Blessed is the one who considers the poor!
> > In the day of trouble the LORD delivers him. (Ps. 41:1)

> Blessed is he who is generous to the poor. (Prov. 14:21)

> Whoever oppresses a poor man insults his Maker. (14:31)

> Whoever is generous to the poor lends to the LORD. (19:17)

> Only, they asked us to remember the poor, the very thing I was eager to do. (Gal. 2:10)

When John the Baptist had second thoughts about whether Jesus was the Messiah, Jesus sent a word back to John: "Go and tell John what you hear and see: the blind receive their sight and the lame walk, lepers are cleansed and the deaf hear, and the dead are raised up, and *the poor have good news preached to them*" (Matt. 11:4–5, emphasis mine).

The same James who told us to dignify trials later rebuked the Jerusalem church for showing favoritism to the rich and dishonoring the poor (James 2:1ff). And when we get to James 5 we find out that he is not finished with this issue. Having warned the Jerusalem church about dishonoring the poor man (2:6), James showed another example about how wealthy Christians in the church had withheld wages to the poor. He echoed the afore-mentioned exact words of Moses warning Israelites to treat the poor with justice and care: "Behold, the wages of the laborers who mowed your fields, which you kept back by fraud, are crying out against you, and the cries of the harvesters have reached the ears of the Lord of hosts" (5:4; cf. Deut. 24:15). God was angry at all this.

Here is what I myself am having to learn. I may think I am pleasing God sufficiently because I read my Bible more, pray more, dignify trials more, and truly forgive those who have hurt me—but then I become satisfied. These "duties"—if that is what they might be called—become almost natural. They no longer take much effort. But making myself remember the poor is not "natu-ral"; I still have to put forth the effort. Therefore, it is dangerous to assume we are making the right decision spiritually when we refrain from doing something because we don't feel "led" in that direction. And dipping deep into our pockets does go against our natural inclination. However, we please God when we go against this inclination and look around to see how much more we can do to help the needy—and do it. I will add one small example: I have been lately convicted that I should tip more when we eat out—at least twenty if not thirty percent. Waiters and waitresses, after all, depend on generous customers for their income. I believe God honors a generous spirit. Indeed, John Wesley once said the last part of a man to be converted is his wallet.

I will now briefly address tithing. Giving God ten percent is merely giving the Lord what is *his* already. The tithe "is the Lord's" (Lev. 27:30); it was required by the Mosaic law (Mal. 3:8–10), endorsed by Jesus (Matt. 23:23), and assumed by Paul (1 Cor.

16:2; 2 Cor. 9:6–9). God has put us on our honor to return to him what he says is his. I have learned this key truth: we cannot outgive the Lord. Having been a tither for over sixty years, I can testify to this. I am not a rich man, but we have always had more than enough to live on. Since I have written a book, *Tithing* (endorsed by Billy Graham and John Stott), I will not elaborate further on this topic. I will only say this, and I don't mean to be unfair: I do not see how it is possible for a Christian to greatly please God if he or she does not tithe consistently.

CHAPTER 9

LIVING THE SERMON ON THE MOUNT

⚜

For I tell you, unless your righteousness exceeds that of the scribes and Pharisees, you will never enter the kingdom of heaven.

—MATTHEW 5:20

If Jesus is only a Teacher, then all He can do is to tantalize us by erecting a standard we cannot come anywhere near. But if we know Him first as Savior, by being born again from above, we know that He did not come to teach us only: He came to make us what He teaches we should be. The Sermon on the Mount is a statement of the life we will live when the Holy Spirit is having His way with us.

—OSWALD CHAMBERS (1874–1917)

L iving out Jesus's teaching in the Sermon on the Mount is the greatest example of pleasing God. But who does this? And what happens if you don't? Does not exceeding the righteousness of the Pharisees mean you cannot go to heaven? What is the kingdom of heaven?

The Sermon on the Mount is the most popular sermon in history. It gets praised by everybody—Christians and non-Christians alike. Sir Winston Churchill (1874–1965) regarded the Sermon on the Mount as the "last word in ethics." President Franklin D. Roosevelt (1882–1945) said, "I doubt if there is any problem in the world today—social, political, or economic—that would not find happy solution if approached in the spirit of the Sermon on the Mount." His successor, Harry S. Truman (1884–1972), said, "I do not believe there is a problem in this country or the world today which could not be settled if approached through the teaching of the Sermon on the Mount."

E. Stanley Jones (1884–1973), a Methodist missionary to India, once asked Mahatma Gandhi (1869–1948), who praised Jesus's teachings, why he did not become a follower of Jesus. Gandhi replied, "I don't reject your Christ. I love your Christ. It is that so many of you Christians are so unlike your Christ." When we get to heaven, we will find out whether Gandhi actually heard the gospel; whether he was told that he was a sinner like everyone else and that his only hope of going to heaven consisted in being sorry for his sins and trusting in the death of Jesus Christ for his salvation. Gandhi is also quoted as saying this: "Oh yes, I am a Christian" based on his own interpretation of the Sermon on the Mount. He especially loved the passage about turning the other cheek when slapped in the face (Matt. 5:39). Dr. Martin Luther

King Jr. (1929–1968) said he got his teaching on passive obedience from Gandhi.

It would be an easy mistake to emphasize Jesus's teaching about human relationships and entirely miss his reason for preaching the Sermon on the Mount. Why did he mention fulfilling the law (v. 17), and what did he mean by the "kingdom of heaven"? This situation reminds me of the comment a liberal friend of mine made after he went with me to hear Dr. Martyn Lloyd-Jones preach. I had told him that Dr. Lloyd-Jones was the greatest preacher since C. H. Spurgeon (who was arguably the greatest in the history of the church). The Doctor was in his best form that night; the anointing of the Spirit was on him powerfully. When the sermon was finished, I turned to my friend.

"Well," I said, "what do you think of that?"

He replied: "Amazing. Just amazing. Not one split infinitive or dangling participle."

Dr. Lloyd-Jones was an old-fashioned Welsh orator; no one was like him. But the power and content of his message went right past my friend. Unfortunately, I think people often do this with Jesus's Sermon on the Mount.

St. Augustine first gave Jesus's teaching in Matthew 5–7 the name "Sermon on the Mount," and this title stuck. This sermon is the passage most referred to in the Bible and possibly the least understood; the best known and the least known. Most people never attempt to get to the bottom of Jesus's teaching. They superficially applaud his words that you should "love your enemies" (5:43–44) and "turn the other cheek" (see v. 39) when mistreated, but do not know why Jesus said these things or how important such teaching is.

Jesus likely took three or four days to teach the Sermon on the Mount. Matthew gives us a summary of the teaching, and Luke repeats some of the same content (e.g., Luke 6:17–49). However, Luke did say the teaching occurred on a plain. A German architect once made a long study of the area and has shown exactly where the Sermon was preached. His conclusion has been recognized by virtually all historians and architects, including the Israeli government. The location is not where the Mount of Beatitudes church lies but is near the Church of the Primacy of St. Peter—a few hundred yards to the east. If you walk up the mountain from the road beside the Sea of Galilee, you will come to a level plain. I have been there several times—it is a flat area covering some three or four hundred yards. The mountain's slope then continues on from there. This explains how Luke could say the people "came down" and were on a "level place" (v. 17). On one of my visits to this location, my friend Lyndon Bowring walked about fifty yards further up the mountain and then sat to listen as I read the Beatitudes. The acoustics were amazing; Lyndon could hear me perfectly. Thousands could easily have been seated in this area and clearly heard every word that Jesus spoke.

Jesus and the Mosaic Law

I explain in my book *The Sermon on the Mount* that the key to understanding the Sermon is to see it as Jesus's application of his doctrine of the Holy Spirit. The Sermon clarifies how Jesus understood the Ten Commandments. When he said that our righteousness must surpass that of the Pharisees, he was not talking about keeping the Ten Commandments outwardly—but inwardly. For instance, the Pharisees kept the seventh commandment outwardly; none would dare physically sleep with another man's wife. But they felt no guilt when they lusted. Jesus consequently clarified that if you lust after a woman, you have committed adultery in your heart (Matt. 5:27ff). One could be a good Pharisee if he only looked and didn't touch. He could be a good Pharisee and hate his enemy—or hold a grudge against someone. After all, the Mosaic law that the Pharisees followed scrupulously was against physical murder. But Jesus taught that anger and unforgiveness were equal to murder (5:21ff, 43ff). A Pharisee could rigidly adhere to the Old Testament teaching about swearing by the name of the Most High God. But Jesus showed that this could go against the spirit of the third commandment, which says, "You shall not take the name of the LORD your God in vain"—that is, misuse his name (Ex. 20:7). So Jesus clarified that one should not swear at all but just utter a simple "yes" or "no" (Matt. 5:33–37).

Jesus turned the Mosaic law upside down without repudiating it. Some thought that Jesus would abolish the law. Some hoped that he would. But no—he instead introduced a much higher standard than outwardly keeping the law. Paul called this the "law of Christ" (1 Cor. 9:21; Gal. 6:2). This is Jesus's interpretation of the Mosaic law in the Sermon on the Mount, which he used to characterize "lusting" as adultery and unforgiveness as murder.

Jesus's disciples failed to grasp the true meaning of the kingdom of heaven during the whole time of his ministry. They never "twigged," to use a British expression—they just didn't get it! Jesus clarified to them that the kingdom of God does not come with observation; that is, the kingdom is not what can be observed outwardly but is within you, "in the midst of you" (Luke 17:20–21). The disciples never got the thought out of their heads that it was only a matter of time until Jesus would overthrow Rome. The truth is, until Pentecost they did not understand why Jesus died. After he was resurrected from the dead they did not know why he died or why he was raised. During the forty-day period following Jesus's resurrection they became frustrated because he would show up, then disappear. Finally, the disciples got their question out—what they wanted to know more than anything—"Lord, will you at this time restore the kingdom to Israel?" (Acts 1:6).

But this was an ill-posed question. Jesus could not possibly answer that question directly with either a "yes" or a "no." It assumed that the disciples' theological prejudice was justified— that Jesus was going to overthrow Caesar. But the truth was, Jesus never came to overthrow Rome! The truth was—and is—that Jesus—the eternal Word made flesh (John 1:14)—came to die, be raised from the dead, and return to his Father to receive the glory he had before the world existed (17:5). He would be seated—a man in glory—at the right hand of the Father as our Intercessor and King. There he would reign until he made all his enemies his footstool (Acts 2:35). His first task as our Intercessor was to pray for the Holy Spirit—the third person of the Godhead—to come down upon those people who tarried in Jerusalem until the day of Pentecost came. He continues to intercede for all those who come to God by him (Heb. 7:25). Finally, a day—known only to the Father—will arrive when Jesus returns to the earth a second time, as the Supreme Judge (Acts 17:31; 2 Thess. 1:5–10).

Just before Jesus ascended to heaven, he said these words to his disciples:

But you will receive power when the Holy Spirit has come upon you, and you will be my witnesses in Jerusalem and in all Judea and Samaria, and to the end of the earth. (Acts 1:8)

The disciples had a lot to think about. Three years of Jesus's ministry, which consisted of teaching and healing, had ended in his death on a Roman cross and then his resurrection from the dead. When Jesus told his disciples not to leave Jerusalem until they had received power from on high, they did not know how long they would have to wait. It turned out to be only ten days. Yet this much is for sure: there was a lot for them to take in. They waited for ten long days not knowing clearly what was happening. Yes, it is likely that the disciples had received a measure of the Spirit on Easter Sunday when Jesus breathed on them and said, "Receive the Holy Spirit" (John 20:22). But it is impossible to know how much this helped them to grasp what was going on— the questions of why Jesus died, why he was raised from the dead, and why he was taken up to heaven remained unanswered. The only thing that apparently happened during those ten days was the disciples' choice of Matthias to replace Judas Iscariot as one of the Twelve (Acts 1:26). Whether they did the right thing there has been debated for centuries.

At last, after these ten days of waiting, the Holy Spirit came down:

When the day of Pentecost arrived, they were all together in one place. And suddenly there came from heaven a sound like a mighty rushing wind, and it filled the entire house where they were sitting. And divided tongues as of fire appeared to them and rested on each one of them. And they were all filled with the Holy Spirit and began to speak in other tongues as the Spirit gave them utterance. (2:1–4)

At that point, things came together for the disciples. For the first time they understood why Jesus came, why he died, why he was raised, and what was happening on that day of Pentecost. Old Testament Scriptures fell into place. The parables of Jesus fell into place. The disciples finally understood the meaning of the kingdom of God. Now they could retroactively understand the Sermon on the Mount, the parables, and other teachings of Jesus. The Holy Spirit made the difference.

WHAT IS THE KINGDOM OF HEAVEN?

The kingdom of heaven is the rule of King Jesus from the right hand of God through the Holy Spirit. (The terms "kingdom of heaven" and "kingdom of God" are used interchangeably.) It is also the reign of the *ungrieved* Spirit of God in the lives of those who have been born again. As I mentioned earlier and will explain in more detail soon, the Holy Spirit can be grieved (Eph. 4:30) and quenched (1 Thess. 5:19). It is impossible for us to live the principles of the Sermon on the Mount without the aid of the ungrieved and unquenched Holy Spirit. The world may admire the Sermon. The Mahatma Gandhis of this world may be in awe of it. But living out the teachings of this sermon is beyond reach for the unsaved and only within reach of those who are born again and also enjoy the rule and reign of the ungrieved Spirit of God.

Hudson Taylor (1832–1905) was a British missionary to China who utterly failed for a good while to reach the people there. He first wore a white suit—but this appeared to annoy the Chinese. Then one day a man riding a bicycle intentionally drove through a mud puddle where Taylor was standing, completely spattering his white suit. Taylor's first response was to go on his knees and pray for that man. He then stopped wearing the white suit and began dressing like the Chinese. From that moment, people by the hundreds came to Christ. In other words, Taylor's practicing the Sermon on the Mount—not merely his preaching—made the difference. Hudson Taylor became a legend.

THE LORD'S PRAYER

The Lord's Prayer appears midway through the Sermon on the Mount (Matt. 6:9–13). It contains six petitions in two parts: (1) God's prayer list concerning himself, and (2) how we should pray for ourselves. Jesus first instructs us to pray the three petitions in the first part, which seek to worship and honor his Father:

1. HALLOWED BE YOUR NAME. The Lord's Prayer is not only a prayer to be prayed but is also a pattern teaching us that we should not rush into God's presence with our needs. Rather, we should first pause to worship him. This both acknowledges the holiness of God's name and expresses our plea that his name will be hallowed and famous all over the world.

2. YOUR KINGDOM COME. Having mentioned the kingdom of heaven several times in the Sermon, Jesus teaches us that we should ask God to send down the ungrieved

Holy Spirit upon our hearts so that he can be resident and real in our lives.

3. YOUR WILL BE DONE, ON EARTH AS IT IS IN HEAVEN. God already has a will of his own; there is no rebellion in heaven among the angels or the sainted dead. In light of this, we welcome God's will to do as he pleases in our lives and gladly accept his wisdom. As Anna Waring put it so beautifully in her hymn, *In Heavenly Love Abiding,*

> He knows the way He taketh,
> And I will walk with Him.

At this stage Jesus lists what our own prayer requests should be. In my book *The Lord's Prayer,* I show that these three requests actually cover every single need we could have.

1. GIVE US THIS DAY OUR DAILY BREAD. This covers our essential physical needs: food, shelter, clothing, sleep, and good health. It is interesting that Jesus puts our physical needs before our spiritual needs. After all, we have to eat; we are not fit to care about spiritual matters when we are starving or unhealthy.

2. FORGIVE US OUR DEBTS, AS WE ALSO HAVE FORGIVEN OUR DEBTORS. This petition is for our spiritual health; it almost certainly guarantees that the Holy Spirit in us will remain ungrieved. But it does put us on the spot! We claim in this prayer that we have forgiven those *who have sinned against us.*

3. LEAD US NOT INTO TEMPTATION, BUT DELIVER US FROM EVIL. The emphasis should be on the word "into";

may God be pleased to spare us from unnecessary testing and trial. We also pray that the devil—our true enemy—will be kept at bay and never have a victory in our lives.

We must never forget that the Lord's Prayer (repeated in Luke 11:2–4) is given in the context of Jesus's teaching about the kingdom of heaven.

I think we should pray the Lord's Prayer daily. As I mentioned earlier, it is not only a pattern of what good praying is; it is also a prayer to be *prayed*. We recited the Lord's Prayer weekly at Westminster Chapel, and Louise and I have prayed it together daily for years. Caution: beware of the Lord's Prayer becoming so routine that you merely repeat the lines without consciously realizing what you are saying to God. There is no virtue in sheer repetition of the Prayer; you can repeat it easily in half a minute. The benediction, "For yours is the kingdom and the power and the glory forever," which is good to repeat, may or may not have been taught by Jesus originally.

Jesus's Teaching regarding Our Priorities

Those people who want to please God will love the teachings of the Sermon on the Mount *and* sincerely try to carry them out. The Sermon ends, as we will see soon, with a warning that those who hear these teachings but do not carry them out will face imminent disaster.

As I have been emphasizing, the wider context of the Lord's Prayer in the Sermon on the Mount is the kingdom of heaven.

The immediate context is Jesus's admonition that we should not do our righteous actions—giving, praying, and fasting—to be seen by people but to receive a reward from God. Jesus poked fun at hypocrites who sounded a trumpet to ensure they would always have a fawning audience each time they contributed to the poor (Matt. 6:2ff). He explained that their sole reward would be this praise from others. Yet to give discreetly so that nobody but God would notice was an action the Father was pleased to reward. This principle was also true for prayer. While hypocrites pray to be admired, Jesus told his followers to pray in secret—not using many words but applying his own suggestion for what a prayer should be like. Then he gave the Lord's Prayer.

Money

Jesus warned against trying to accumulate wealth on earth but encouraged us to "lay up for yourselves treasures in heaven" (v. 20). We should also not be anxious about lacking food, shelter, and clothing, but seeking first the kingdom of God and his righteousness guarantees that our needs will be supplied (vv. 25–34).

Prayer

Having warned his followers earlier about praying to be seen by people, Jesus encouraged them to be persistent in prayer. We are to keep asking, seeking, and knocking—never ever giving up (7:7–9)! At the end of the day the Father will answer all who ask, seek, and knock.

Practical Holiness

If we want to avoid being judged by others, we must not judge others. We should judge ourselves first, and only judge others when we have completely rid ourselves of any malady (vv. 1–5). The best way to live is to do unto others as you would want them to do to you (v. 12). As Jesus acknowledged, his way is narrow and hard: "those who find it are few" (v. 14). However, those who obey his teachings will find themselves safe when a powerful storm comes; for these teachings are like a rock providing security for those who build upon it. Yet those who hear Jesus's words but do not carry them out will inevitably have a great fall (vv. 24–27).

FALSE PROPHETS

We must beware of people who outwardly appear innocent but inwardly are "ravenous wolves." They can be recognized by their "fruits." Jesus did not say specifically what these fruits are, but presumably these people are exposed when their prophecies do not come true. They may have done mighty works and even cast out demons, but they have not known Jesus's Father and will be rejected on the last day (vv. 15–23).

AUTHORITY AND POWER

Matthew immediately records the effect the Sermon on the Mount had on the crowds; they were "astonished" (Gr. *exeplessonto*— "amazed"). What impressed the people was Jesus's "authority" (Gr. *exousian*—"power," the kind of power and authority Pontius Pilate had to order Jesus's crucifixion [see John 19:10]). In other words, when the Jewish scribes spoke, apparently no one was particularly moved one way or the other. Their hearers could take or leave the scribes' words without sensing any obligation to believe them. But when Jesus spoke, the people were gripped: shaken, moved. "No one ever spoke like this man!" (7:46).

Jesus, a man who sought only to please his Father, spoke in a way that would have pleased the Father: the people were shaken rigid by his words. Not all who read this book will be preachers, teachers, or ministers. But surely any Christian layperson reading this would want to believe with "full assurance of understanding" (Col. 2:2—Gr. *plerophoria*)—that is, when you know without doubt that you have got it right. I say to you, dear reader—minister or not—God would be pleased if you *believe with the same confidence and authority* that described Jesus when he spoke. *Jesus believed the words he spoke.* This is so important. How many of us truly believe in our heart of hearts what we claim—that we would go to the stake for what we say? There are countless people in ministry who privately ask themselves, "Is this really true?"

My dad once asked a well-known holiness preacher, "Brother Fleming, do we have the truth?" Rev. Bona Fleming replied, "We have some of it." Dad told me this story, and it has always stuck with me.

On October 12, 1740, George Whitefield preached in the Boston Common to twenty-three thousand people. Benjamin Franklin (1706–1790) was in the crowd. Someone asked Franklin, "Do you believe what Whitefield is saying?" He replied, "I don't know, but he certainly does."

I remember sharing an incident that showed God's power with a close ministerial friend of mine. He immediately responded, "That means what we preach is real and true!"—and I agreed.

William Booth, founder of the Salvation Army, began his address to the first graduating class of officers with these words: "Perhaps I should apologize, brothers and sisters, for keeping you here for two years just to teach you how to lead a soul to Christ. Far better had you spent five minutes in hell." In that scenario, no one would then have to teach these students. Having seen the torments of hell, the graduates would speak with awe and authority. Their conviction would be shown by the look on their faces. The tone in their voices. The content of their words. They would be a reliable witness to the truth. Their hearers would know they were not making it up.

Jesus had this same conviction when he spoke. It is what Peter wants us to have: "Whoever speaks, as one who speaks oracles of God" (1 Pet. 4:11). Stephen's opponents were powerless against that conviction: "They could not withstand the wisdom and the Spirit with which he was speaking" (Acts 6:10). Finally, "Now when [the Sanhedrin] saw the boldness of Peter and John, and perceived that they were uneducated, common men, they were astonished. And they recognized that they had been with Jesus" (4:13).

I strongly believe that God wants you and me to live out the teachings of the Sermon on the Mount. This would please him. I equally believe that God wants you and me to *believe the words* of Jesus with the same conviction and honesty that Jesus had when he spoke. If we do, the world will once again see that there is a God in the heavens who is in control and who holds our destinies in his hands.

May God hasten the day when this characterizes you and me.

CHAPTER 10

BE SENSITIVE TO
THE HOLY SPIRIT

❧

And do not grieve the Holy Spirit of God, by whom you were sealed for the day of redemption. Let all bitterness and wrath and anger and clamor and slander be put away from you, along with all malice. Be kind to one another, tender-hearted, forgiving one another, as God in Christ forgave you.
—EPHESIANS 4:30–32

There is no worse screen to block out the Spirit than confidence in our own intelligence.
—JOHN CALVIN (1509–1564)

I had an overwhelming experience of the Lord's presence. I felt so powerfully overcome by the nearness of the Holy Spirit that I had to ask the Lord to draw back lest He kill me. It was so glorious that I couldn't stand more than a small portion of it.
—MORDECAI HAM (1877–1961)

Christianity, as we know it, is what it is because of Tertullian (c. 155–220). Known as both the father of Latin Christianity and the founder of Christian theology in the Western world, he originated the word "Trinity." Tertullian used the Latin word *trinitas* to refer to the Father, Son, and Holy Spirit together. When referring to each member of the Godhead, he used the Latin term *persona*. God the Father is a person. Jesus Christ, the Son of God, is a person. The Holy Spirit is God and is a person. In this last chapter, I want to focus on being sensitive to the person of the Holy Spirit and why this needs to happen if we are truly to please God. In a few words: The New Testament teaches us that lives worth living are in harmony with the Spirit.

The Holy Spirit is a very, very sensitive person. He can be grieved (Eph. 4:30). He can be quenched (1 Thess. 5:19). He can be blasphemed (Matt. 12:31). He can be lied to (Acts 5:3). He can be resisted (7:51). He can give clear direction (8:29; 16:6–7). When I first submitted the manuscript that became *Sensitivity of the Spirit* to my British publisher, I wanted to call the book *The Hypersensitivity of the Spirit*. They talked me out of this, fearing that readers would not understand. I can see why they said that.

When we refer to a person as "hypersensitive," this is not a compliment. We may say, "You have to walk on eggshells with that person," knowing that his or her feelings get hurt very easily and quickly. So, "hypersensitive" is not a positive thing to say about a person, but—like it or not—*that is the way the Holy Spirit is*. He is a very sensitive person; he gets his feelings hurt easily. When Paul said, "Do not *grieve* the Holy Spirit of God," he used the Greek word *lupeite*, which can mean "to get your feelings hurt." You may find yourself saying, "He ought to not be like that!" But this indeed happens to be the way he is! In more detail, *lupeite* means "to distress, to make sorrowful, to affect with sadness." Imagine this: we can make the Holy Spirit feel sad. We do know that Jesus had feelings. He was furious when he saw the money-changers in the temple (John 2:14ff). He wept over the city of Jerusalem (Luke 19:41). In Gethsemane he said, "My soul is very sorrowful" (Matt. 26:38). The Holy Spirit took Jesus's place, referring to himself as "another Helper" (Gr. *allon parakleton*, which means "one who comes alongside"; translated variously as "Comforter," "Advocate," or "Helper"). Jesus had been precisely a Helper to the disciples for some three years. "Another" person—who would also have feelings just like Jesus—would now take his place and be with them forever (John 14:16).

I choose not to enter the subject of the impassibility of God—the doctrine that God cannot be moved by emotion. Some will ask, "How can the Holy Spirit be grieved if God the Father is impassible?" Some might also ask, "How can the Holy Spirit be quenched if God's grace is irresistible?" I answer as lovingly as I know how, having been a preacher for sixty-five years: we need to be governed by Holy Scripture rather than logic. If we are governed by logic, then God is the author of sin—which he isn't. How do we know he isn't? Because the Word says so! How do we know God can be grieved? Because Ephesians 4:30 says so. I have chosen to camp at the burning bush. When God says "STOP," I want to stop. And take off my shoes. And just worship. I don't want to be unfair, but I suspect that those who want to figure everything out get into all kinds of trouble and miss what God may want to teach them.

We must now answer two questions: (1) What grieves the Holy Spirit? and (2) What happens when we grieve the Spirit?

What Grieves the Holy Spirit?

Anything that displeases God grieves the Holy Spirit, for the Holy Spirit is God. For some reason Paul mentions bitterness first; it is an *attitude* that grieves the Spirit. This means that I must recognize that when I feel bitter, like it or not, agree or disagree: the Holy Spirit is *grieved*. I must learn to be honest with myself and not imagine that I am an exception to this rule. If I am bitter, I should know at once that the Spirit is sad. Then Paul lists wrath, anger, clamor, slander, and all malice. Everything comes to this: unforgiveness. I may initially deny that I need to forgive, but sooner or later I must accept that *when* I feel vindictive, *when* I am upset, *when* I start shouting, or *when* I say something that may damage a person's reputation or want to get even with a person, *the Spirit of God is grieved*. It may take a month, it may take a year, or it may take five minutes, but I will eventually have to bow to the word of God that says I have grieved the Holy Spirit.

Ephesians 4 and 5 is the main place where Paul brings up the topic of grieving the Spirit. He even gave us a list covering what grieves the Spirit in Ephesians 5: sexual immorality, all impurity, covetousness, filthiness, foolish talk, and crude joking. Those who practice these things have "no *inheritance* in the kingdom of Christ and God" (vv. 3–5, emphasis mine). Does this mean that they are not saved? No—but please feel free to review what I said about inheritance in chapter 5.

You may recall that I said near the beginning of this book— words that I choose to repeat: "Find out what grieves the Holy Spirit and don't do that; you have your work cut out for you."

Strange as this may seem, grieving the Holy Spirit is the easiest thing in the world to do. We often have no awareness that we grieved him. It is a bit like Samson's sin of giving his secret to Delilah; he didn't feel a thing when he did this. "He did not know that the Lord had left him" (Judg. 16:20). But Samson soon found out that he was as weak as any man; his anointing of physical strength was gone. In much the same way, when we feel angry it seems right. As I said earlier, any backslider is filled with his own ways (Prov. 14:14). Whenever we lose our temper, hold a grudge, or point a finger, we feel justified in that moment.

I like to define spirituality this way: *closing the time gap between sin and repentance.* How long does it take you to realize or admit you were wrong? Some say, "I will never admit I was wrong." Some take years. Some cool off after a few months. Some do it in weeks. Some in days. Some in hours. Some even in seconds. If you can narrow the time gap to seconds, you are possibly getting closer to knowing God's "ways." God lamented that the people of ancient Israel "have not known my ways" (Heb. 3:10). We may not like his ways. But he is the only true God! We must adjust to him; he will not adjust to us.

The Holy Spirit will not bend the rules for any of us. In my book *Prophetic Integrity*, I shared a personal story about when I lost my temper with Louise. Time was critical because I had a major sermon to prepare—but I got nowhere in the wake of our argument. My knowledge, my experience, my understanding, my pleading with God, and my feeling of desperation got me *nowhere*. Not a single valid thought came. After seven hours of trying to get a sermon, I had made absolutely no progress. To paraphrase Calvin, our dependence on our intelligence is a sure screen to blocking the Spirit. But the moment I apologized to Louise, everything changed. In less than forty-five minutes I had everything I needed for a complete sermon.

You can accomplish more in five minutes when the Spirit of God is not grieved than you can in five years when you try twisting God's arm.

I repeat: God will not bend the rules for any of us. He is no respecter of persons—whether you have been a Christian for fifty years or are a bishop, pastor, teacher, or another high-profile person in the church. God wants us to know *his* ways. One of the ways of the Spirit, then, is that he can be easily grieved. Again, you might say, "He ought to not be like that!" But that is the way he is. You need to accept this.

What Happens When We Grieve the Holy Spirit

What happens when we make the Holy Spirit sad or hurt his feelings? How serious is it if we grieve him? Right away, I do want to make a critical point about what, thankfully, does *not* happen when we grieve the Spirit: *We do not lose the Holy Spirit when we grieve him.* After all, Jesus said that the Spirit would abide with us "forever" (John 14:16). He also said, "I am with you always" (Matt. 28:20) and "I will never leave you nor forsake you" (Heb. 13:5). In English, a double negative such as "I don't never" is bad grammar. But the Greek language allows a double negative—an equivalent Greek phrase, translated into proper English, would read: "I will never, never leave you." Actually, it really means, "I will never, never, never, never, never, never, never leave you!" God "*sealed* [us] for the day of redemption" (Eph. 4:30, emphasis mine).

Sealed. We are loved "with an everlasting love" (Jer. 31:3), which God wants us to embrace. Although grieving the Spirit is in some measure a kind of backsliding, it does not necessarily set you on a downward spiral and mean you will backslide disgracefully.

You may wonder about Jesus's words on the unforgiveable sin, blasphemy against the Spirit (Matt. 12:31–32). The blasphemy of the Spirit is refusing to affirm the witness of the Spirit about Jesus—namely, that Jesus is God. Many sincere Christians worry that they have committed the unpardonable sin. If you, dear reader, worry about this, I ask you: Can you say from the bottom of your heart that *JESUS IS GOD*? If so, I assure you: worry no more, worry no more. Only those speaking in the Holy Spirit can say that Jesus is Lord and God (1 Cor. 12:3).

That said, when we grieve the Spirit we need to *immediately*—or as soon as possible—recognize this and seek forgiveness as soon as possible. Otherwise, we will be wedded to bitterness and unforgiveness and consequently deprive ourselves from having a close relationship to God. We may not realize this for a while. We get used to it. We fall asleep spiritually. You don't know you were asleep until you wake up; you do things when you are asleep (e.g., in your dreams) which you would not do when awake. For instance, I was totally betrayed by my closest friend and mentor many years ago. I became entrenched in hurt, anger, and sorrowful feelings for myself and was left in a somber emotional state for years. I was traumatized and needed counseling. Mercifully, God never left me—but a long time passed before I got right in myself. I was the loser for all those years. Grieving the Spirit and failing to repent of it also has major relevance to our inheritance, which we examined back in chapter 5.

Another important thing happens when we grieve the Holy

Spirit: we lose the *sense* of his presence. We don't lose his presence; we lose our *awareness* of his presence. We risk forfeiting the anointing of the Spirit—and almost certainly lose his *conscious anointing*. We forget what the joy of our salvation was like; we forget what inner peace was like. We lose clear thinking. We become murmurers, grumblers, and complainers. We don't enjoy reading our Bibles. We postpone prayer time. We certainly don't talk to the unsaved about Jesus. We wonder how we could ever have been so excited about spiritual things. We lack gentleness—we find fault with everything and everybody. People then become nervous around us. We become quite unteachable and are usually unreachable.

CONSIDER THE ANALOGY OF THE DOVE

John the Baptist told us how he knew that Jesus was God's Messiah. Please read these words carefully:

> I saw the Spirit descend from heaven like a dove, and it remained on him. I myself did not know him, but he who sent me to baptize with water said to me, "He on whom you see the Spirit descend and remain, this is he who baptizes with the Holy Spirit." And I have seen and have borne witness that this is the Son of God. (John 1:32–34)

Many of us remember the reference to the dove, which has become a symbol of the Holy Spirit. We see the dove imprinted in stained glass windows in church buildings and we see pictures and paintings of doves in Christian literature and art.

The dove is a very shy bird—a wild bird. You cannot get close to a dove without it flying away. The dove is gentle, loving, and peaceful. It barely makes a sound—only a soft and sweet "coo, coo." You probably won't find a dove where there are lots of people or lots of traffic. You will more likely see a dove in a park where there are trees or outside of town.

Pigeons and doves are in the same family. Anatomically they are the same—their bones and organs are identical. But temperamentally they are not the same. You cannot train a dove; you can train a pigeon. Doves are gentle; pigeons are boisterous. Doves are loving; pigeons get angry. You will not likely reach down and pick up a dove; but I have a photograph of our son T. R. with four pigeons on each arm and two on his head! In my book *Pigeon Religion*, I list nineteen differences between a pigeon and a dove. I have also observed that just as many people cannot tell the difference between a pigeon and a dove, neither do some recognize the authentic Holy Spirit in church. "We had a fantastic service—the Holy Ghost came down in power," one says. But when you find out more about what happened, you realize it was probably pigeon religion. The pigeon is the counterfeit Holy Spirit. For instance, some take noise as proof of the Spirit's presence. Not that the Holy Spirit cannot bring noise—great noise, indeed. Yes. But one can work up noise and think that the Holy Spirit is at work. No—you cannot work up the Spirit's presence. Furthermore, he may show up in more than one way. His presence may cause worship. This can create great joy—even shouting. It may bring a deep sense of the fear of God—of awe. The Spirit's presence may also cause healing—when people are healed right, left, and center! Or the Spirit could bring immense quietness upon everyone, so that they do not want to move. I think that some believe the spiritual gift of discerning the spirits or "distinguish[ing] between spirits" (1 Cor. 12:10) refers mainly to the demonic. But it also means discerning the genuine presence of the Holy Spirit of God.

Please reread the Scripture quoted earlier—John 1:32ff. The word "dove" always leaps out. Did you also notice the word "remain"? It is there *twice*! The Holy Spirit came down on Jesus and "remained" on him. I have to admit that when the Spirit descends on me—and thank God this has happened—he doesn't remain. When the Spirit is present, the feeling is wonderful. Indescribable. God is so real. Everything seems in place. You realize that God is in control. You may say to yourself, "After this moment, I will never doubt God again." But hours later the atmosphere is different. Life goes on. The peace and joy diminish. What happened?

Here is what almost certainly happened: the dove flew away. He does not remain. Why did the dove leave? He may need no reason. Isaiah discovered it, and you will also discover it: "Truly, you are a God who hides himself" (Isa. 45:15). This is one of God's "ways." Or perhaps we have grieved him—such as when we speak curtly to someone, are rude on the phone, are impatient while driving, or give an audible exasperated sigh because the person in the checkout line ahead of us is in no hurry. The dove clearly hears all of these complaints. I'm sorry, but God doesn't bend the rules for us just because we have spent a good while in prayer. Our relationship with the Spirit goes on sixty seconds a minute all day long.

Maintaining the *abiding presence* of the ungrieved Spirit is the greatest challenge I have ever experienced in my lifetime.

Sometimes it doesn't seem fair. You are doing your best, when suddenly something unpleasant happens. Someone you are with is unreasonable, and you struggle to stay calm and pleasant. You look forward to a picnic, and it rains. You can't wait for Christmas, but someone doesn't like the present you gave—or is sick and can't celebrate with you. You wait in line at the airport for an important engagement and the plane is late—or the flight is canceled. On more than one occasion, I have stepped inside the train or plane just in time for the doors to shut one second later—an extremely anxious moment. One time my plane from Nashville to Fort Worth was late, and T. R. and I nearly missed our plane to Seoul, South Korea. We *ran* from Terminal Three to Terminal Four, arriving just as they were closing the door. "STOP!" we shouted. Thankfully, we were able to walk on board, the door closed behind us, and the plane took off. Did I grieve the Spirit in my anxiety? Maybe not. Paul said not to be "anxious about *anything*" (Phil. 4:6, emphasis mine), but this can seem impossible to do at times. There is, I think, often a thin line between what grieves the Spirit and what God winks at. If you say that it is ridiculous even to talk about this, I answer: Not to grieve the Holy Spirit is the greatest challenge I know of, and I don't want to get this wrong. Yes, it can seem unfair and unreasonable to try not to be anxious or get angry. But after many years of practicing the presence of God like this, I remind myself that I am so privileged to know the Lord in the first place! I don't need to understand everything. Like Moses before the burning bush (Ex. 3:5–6), there are some things God does not want us to figure out.

I have never yet regretted trying too hard to not grieve the Spirit. But I have too often regretted not trying and instead giving in to my natural feelings.

Does God not understand? Of course he does. Paul admits to being virtually a nervous wreck in 2 Corinthians 2 when he couldn't find Titus. He was so worried about Titus that he even turned down an open door where he could preach the gospel (vv. 12–13). (How many of us preachers would become this vulnerable and admit we had a chance to preach but turned it down because we were too preoccupied with a personal concern?) Did Paul grieve the Spirit during this time? Possibly. Did Paul grieve the Spirit when he angrily called the Jewish high priest "you whitewashed wall!" (Acts 23:3)? What say you? Remember this: Paul wasn't Jesus.

Is there a difference between grieving the Spirit and quenching the Spirit? Grieving the Spirit is what we can do to the Spirit *in* us. Quenching the Spirit is what we might do when the Spirit is at work *outside* us. I can thwart the Spirit's working when he wants to bless others. For example, I can quench the Spirit when I discourage you from affirming what God is clearly doing. I can pour cold water on people who have been enthralled by what God is doing in their church or in their lives. And I can demoralize sincere Christians who are overjoyed with God's presence by making fun of them or making them feel stupid.

The Greek word for "abide" and "remain" are the same, deriving from the root word *meno*. For instance, the Holy Spirit chose to "remain" on Jesus. I think the Spirit came down on him and stayed put, saying, "I like it here; I am at home." Jesus never—ever—grieved the Holy Spirit. He later told his disciples to "abide"—remain—in him (John 15:7). In this case, we must make the choice to abide. Yes, it is a challenge! It is an act of the will.

What is it like when the Holy Spirit is in us *ungrieved*? When he is *unquenched*? We may actually feel nothing. After all, regeneration is an unconscious work of the Spirit. If you say, "I know the day and the hour and the place where I was born again," I know what you mean. But it is more likely that you remember a time of great assurance of being saved. As conception takes place nine months before natural birth, regeneration—bringing a conviction of sin and awareness of our lost condition—may begin a good while before we consciously receive the Lord.

Sometimes the Holy Spirit can be *felt* unmistakably. This sometimes happens at conversion, but it can also happen after conversion. Mordecai Ham's experience (quoted at the beginning of this chapter) of being so overwhelmed that he feared imminent death came after he had been a Christian for a while. D. L. Moody (1837–1899) testified that he had unexpectedly received the same kind of experience as he was walking in Brooklyn. Like Ham, he asked God to "stray His hand" lest he die. Dr. Lloyd-Jones reckoned that the Galatians *felt something* when Paul asked, "Did you receive the Spirit by works of the law or by hearing with faith?" (Gal. 3:2). After all, how would they know they had "received" the Spirit if they had not felt him when he came?

When the Holy Spirit is ungrieved in me—which is something I want all the time—I usually feel nothing at all. When I pray, read my Bible, sing, and wait before God, I usually feel nothing. But times come—so sweet and impossible to describe—when, for example, a joyful feeling or a *thought* regarding a verse in the Bible unexpectedly emerges. I then put everything aside, quickly turn to my computer, and start writing! This is how I write sermons— and books. This book also.

I had the privilege of knowing Oral Roberts before he died, having been in his California home three times. He once said to me, "Do nothing until you feel the anointing." I knew what he meant. By the way, Oral prayed for Louise. When he put his hand on her head, she could hardly stand—I had to hold her. The anointing of the Spirit is truly special and powerful.

Why is this subject important? Abiding in the presence of the ungrieved Spirit pleases God. And he pleases those who do this. It is the best way to live.

Spiritual Gifts Please God

I have one more thing to mention. Paul mentions nine spiritual gifts (1 Cor. 12:8–10). How do they fit into pleasing God? Answer: Paul said we should earnestly desire the "higher gifts" (v. 31). This phrase is a dead giveaway that some gifts are more important than others. It is possible that Paul begins with the most important gift, but that is only my supposition. Moreover, seeking and desiring spiritual gifts is a way to please God.

1. WISDOM. This heads the list: the ability to see something in advance which you will be glad you said or did. Wisdom is saying the right thing at the right time. It consists in knowing the next step forward in God's will for your life.
2. KNOWLEDGE. This could either mean solid theological wisdom or possibly having a "word of knowledge"—helping people to see God's word for them.
3. FAITH. This is not justifying faith or even persevering faith, but rather a special gift for a unique occasion, especially in an emergency.
4. HEALING. This is an endowment by the Spirit to physically or spiritually heal people, possibly by the laying on of hands.
5. MIRACLES. This gift could certainly include healing, but may also cover the deliverance of people from demons.

6. PROPHECY. This is a supernatural ability to know God's will for the moment, and possibly in foretelling the future.
7. DISCERNMENT. This is being able to recognize the true presence of the Holy Spirit vis-à-vis the counterfeit, and may also include the ability to recognize the demonic.
8. TONGUES. This is the ability to speak or pray in a language not your own.
9. INTERPRETATION OF TONGUES. This is the ability to interpret the words or meaning of speech or prayer in a language not your own.

Do you need the gifts of the Spirit to please God? I answer: You need to be *willing* to have any gift of the Spirit to please him. But you have these spiritual gifts because God is pleased with you, not because you are pleasing him. Since gifts are irrevocable and without repentance (Rom. 11:29), they are no sure sign of pleasing God. But I repeat: your *willingness* to have any of these gifts is a prerequisite to pleasing him.

Are these gifts of the Spirit available today? Of course, they are. "Jesus Christ is the same yesterday and today and forever" (Heb. 13:8). The Holy Spirit is also the same yesterday and today and forever.

Pleasing God, then, comes to this: pray to be filled with the Spirit. Also pray that your deepest desire is to please him. "Delight yourself in the LORD, and he will give you the desires of your heart" (Ps. 37:4). If you pray to please God, he will show you the next step forward in how to please him. And when you find a way to please him that you had not thought of before, seize it! Run with it. Use the gifts that the ungrieved Spirit distributes throughout the church. And remind God of his own word! Indeed, John

Calvin said that the best way to pray is to remind God of his own promise. For example, when our son T. R. says to me, "But, Daddy, you promised!" my heart is melted. And our Heavenly Father is the perfect father: "No good thing does he withhold from those who walk uprightly" (Ps. 84:11).

CONCLUSION

I choose to conclude with three brief statements that summarize what I have endeavored to say in this book. Everything comes down to these points:

1. Pleasing God is accomplished by obeying and dwelling in the ungrieved Spirit of God.
2. Pleasing God is what guarantees coming into your inheritance, ensuring his "Well done!" approval at the judgment seat of Christ.
3. The chief way we please God is to affirm his word to the hilt, to find out what grieves the Holy Spirit and not doing that.

There is no greater inner satisfaction on this planet than the clear knowledge that you please God. It simply does not get better than this. No amount of money, fame, friendship, or success can dignify the way God made us—namely, that we might live to please him. As St. Augustine put it, our hearts are restless until they find their repose in God.

Pleasing God gives you that rest.

May the blessing of God the Father, God the Son, and God the Holy Spirit, together with the sprinkling of the blood of Jesus, be with you and abide with you now and evermore. Amen.

Prophetic Integrity: Aligning Our Words with God's Word

R. T. Kendall (Foreword by Dr. Michael L. Brown)

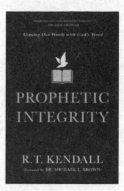

What happens when prophets are wrong?

In 2020, many Christians claiming to be prophets said God had told them that Donald Trump would be reelected as president. Over thirty years earlier, Paul Cain, one of the famous Kansas City Prophets, had prophesied that there would be a revival in London in 1990, which never came to pass. These examples make us wonder:

- What happens when prophets get it wrong?
- Are there consequences for misleading God's people?
- What would a genuine prophet look like today?
- How can you tell a false prophet from a genuine one?

In recent years, misjudgments among charismatic Christians claiming to speak for God as well as moral failures within evangelicalism have resulted in a crisis of belief. In *Prophetic Integrity*, bestselling author and speaker R. T. Kendall gives a warning to those speaking in God's name and offers a way forward in trusting God despite the failures of the church.